improving
reading research

Edited by
Roger Farr
Samuel Weintraub
Bruce Tone

INTERNATIONAL READING ASSOCIATION
800 Barksdale Road   Newark, Delaware 19711

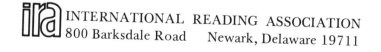

Copyright 1976 by the
International Reading Association, Inc.

Library of Congress Cataloging in Publication Data

Main entry under title:

Improving reading research.

Papers from the International Reading Association's preconvention institute on research held in New Orleans.
Includes bibliographies.
1. Reading research—Congresses.
I. Farr, Roger C. II. Weintraub, Samuel, 1927-
III. Tone, Bruce. IV. International Reading Association.
LB1050.6.I46   428'.4'072   76-795
ISBN 0-87207-484-6
Second Printing, May 1977

Contents

Foreword   *v*

1   Introduction
      Samuel Weintraub
      Roger Farr

8   Identifying and planning reading research
      Helen M. Robinson

23   Design problems in reading research
      James L. Wardrop

34   Measurement issues in reading research
      Harold F. Bligh

45   Conducting longitudinal research in reading
      Kathryn A. Blake
      Jerry C. Allen

71   Interpreting the findings: some cautions
      Albert J. Harris

81   Linguistics in reading research
      Ronald Wardhaugh

89   Linguistically sound research in reading
      Kenneth S. Goodman

101   Social aspects of working with the schools
      Nicholas J. Anastasiow

109   Reporting: the last major step in the research act
      Bruce Tone

The International Reading Association attempts, through its publications, to provide a forum for a wide spectrum of opinion on reading. This policy permits divergent viewpoints without assuming the endorsement of the Association.

Foreword

Somewhere, one of the sages has written, "Nothing is so powerful as an idea whose time has come." This statement applies clearly to the IRA Board's voting in 1965 to establish the *Reading Research Quarterly*.

True, we had an alert and perceptive Board—one which could take a long-term view and see that the Association had the clear obligation to provide an official IRA outlet for serious, lengthy papers which explored research problems deeply and insightfully—problems which were practical, theoretical, and sophisticated.

As president of the Association at the time of the approval of the founding of the *Quarterly*, I will admit to "good words in its favor spoken in smoke-filled rooms." Although at times I have heard Ralph Staiger's mind click like a taxi meter—and aren't we fortunate for his long guidance in financial and professional matters?—he did support the idea of the *Quarterly*, which was likely to appear on the negative side of the Association's financial ledger.

So a happy circumstance of the times, an enlightened Board and a sympathetic Executive Director, led to the founding of IRA's third journal and also set the Association's course on a publication program which is today massive, diversified, and distinguished.

As the first editor of the *Quarterly*, I am proud of how far we have come, of the excellent subsequent editors who improved and expanded our original concept of the *Quarterly*. And I am proud that the Association has accepted its responsibility to serve the members with a variety of publications.

Ten years from now we will have moved in new, important directions in all of our publications, which will have even greater usefulness to our members. There is no question of this. There can be no question of this.

The series of papers of this volume from the New Orleans Preconvention Institute on Research result in a document which merits the attention of all members of the Association. It marks the tenth volume year of the *Quarterly* and is another significant contribution to the literature by IRA.

THEODORE CLYMER
Founding Editor, *Reading Research Quarterly*
Director, Institute for Reading Research,
Santa Barbara

Introduction

SAMUEL WEINTRAUB
State University of New York at Buffalo
ROGER FARR
Indiana University

   This volume on improving reading research focuses on basic design questions which too often flaw research. A lack of attention to fundamentals—not to esoteric or sophisticated concerns—accounts for much that has been weak in research. These basics should be second nature to the experienced researcher, but too often they are not. And they should be emphasized for the neophyte researcher so that he can sharpen his skills. The purpose of this volume is to focus on the fundamentals in an effort to improve future research conducted by both the experienced researcher and the neophyte.

   A review of numerous studies on who conducts research indicates that frequently a researcher conducts only one study. Too often the quest of the budding investigator gets nipped, and the dissertation stands as the sole research contribution. Occasionally a research effort follows the dissertation, but then the investigator's name disappears from the research literature. The bulk of research, then, is done by one-time researchers, and the members of the reading profession who continuously pursue and report research efforts constitute a distressingly small number.

   One would assume that the experienced researcher would produce a better effort than the neophyte. At least it makes sense that experience in any area is a powerful teacher. No one has really studied this thesis, and so we do not *know* that such is the case. It may be that if the beginning researcher is careless he continues to produce sloppy efforts, showing little or no improvement; but one would hope that one way to improve research would be through continued practice in doing it while sharpening the researcher's thinking skills.

Another avenue toward improving research efforts is to make the first efforts of the neophyte better. Even if it is his only effort, a general improvement of reading research would result. This volume should be valuable for the beginning researcher. That includes the graduate student who is in search of a dissertation topic as well as the student at the stage of developing his proposal and the student preparing to write his final report. It includes the post doctoral researcher thinking about his first independently planned research and perhaps even the more sophisticated worker who has already produced several investigations but still feels the need to sharpen his basic research skills. The volume is addressed to all researchers who understand the need to make their efforts more credible.

Does reading research need to improve?

Since William S. Gray first began abstracting and annotating the reading research literature in 1925, about 9,000 published reports have been identified. It would seem that every aspect of reading has surely been investigated with marked thoroughness. And certainly with so many published reports extant, all of our questions should have been answered.

Regrettably, such is not the case; unanswered questions abound. And criticisms of the research are not at all unusual. Gray (1950) noted that the research was fragmentary. In reviewing the publications on phonic programs, Chall (1967) remarked that the research in that area was disappointingly inconclusive. She attributed her conclusion to the poor quality of the research she reviewed. Others have made similar statements relative to reading research, and the documentation of such statements would include dozens of references.

The *Reading Research Quarterly* annually accepts for publication about one out of every 8-10 manuscripts received. Most of those not published are rejected because of a lack of attention to the fundamentals of good research. The design may be inappropriate, the statistical techniques incorrect, the tests invalid, the sample poor, or the study so basically flawed in any number of other ways as to be of very limited value. Some of the studies rejected by the *Quarterly* have appeared in print elsewhere without having been improved upon—their flaws remain.

The continued publication of seriously flawed research probably does more harm than good to the profession. Although a poor study may have one or more elements of merit, it is, nevertheless, still poor and probably should not appear in print—at least not without an accompanying critique. The editors of journals and the advisory board members on refereed journals share the responsibility for seeing that minimum standards of quality are met. The publication of weak research simply encourages further production of the same. There is no need to improve if one is rewarded for inappropriate questions, flawed designs, and fuzzy thinking.

The many criticisms of published research, the very few definite conclusions that can be drawn from the numerous studies reported, the high number of rejections by not just the *Quarterly* but other publications, all suggest that the need to improve the quality of the research literature is not only a worthwhile undertaking but an imperative need.

What is research?

In an editorial statement, we defined research as a way of thinking (*Reading Research Quarterly*, Vol. X, No. 1). It is the sharpening and clarification of this thinking to which the papers in this volume address themselves. Wardrop emphasizes that good research begins with asking good questions. Asking good questions is another way of thinking clearly. Perhaps we have done little of the latter in our past research efforts—or at least not enough of it.

In her paper, Robinson raises a point that precedes Wardrop's need for asking a good question. She implies that a good research question can only be developed from an extensive knowledge base. Good research, then, begins with a scholarly grasp of an area. It does not develop from an intuition or a visceral feeling. The intuition may have been the conception, but before the final delivery of the worthwhile questions, much incubation must take place. Unlike Athena, a study does not appear full-blown from the head of the researcher. The development of a worthwhile question might thus be analogous to the fetal stage of the infant. And 9 months from conception to delivery may even be an underestimate of the time needed for a well-developed question to be born. Only the individual who knows what has been done can know what yet needs to be done.

Wardhaugh reminds us that becoming proficient in linguistics is no easy task; and Goodman suggests that the parallel is true in reading. Although many authors discourse as if they were experts in the area, their understanding is often quite limited. *Good* research in reading must have as its basis a solid understanding of at least the area under investigation, and the essential relevance between linguistics and reading exemplifies how better research can result from a broader knowledge base from several areas in reading.

Most of the papers in this volume deal with but one type of research—the classical empirical design. This emphasis seems valid because the vast preponderance of research literature that has been done and that continues to be produced follows the classical model. The emphasis is upon statistical procedures, and the outline tends to follow relatively well established stages. Tone gives an overview of these steps in his chapter as well as thoughtful considerations for the writing of each.

Research, however, is—or ought to be—more broadly defined than the classical type model. It seems crucial that we begin to look at other types of research and recognize them as respectable. Wardrop, Wardhaugh, and Robinson either refer to other types of research or at least imply the need for searching out other types. Robinson mentions historical and case study, among others. We would like to suggest the need for going beyond even these recognized—albeit not always "respectable"—forms. It is time that we searched for new models to follow or developed our own. As noted in another editorial statement, methodological incarceration has afflicted us (*Reading Research Quarterly*, X, No. 4).

The fractionation that has developed in our search for the reading process and in the various research efforts that have attempted to resolve some of our methodology problems may be directly attributable to the use of inappropriate research models. In our efforts to gain academic respectability in the eyes of allied professions, we have adopted models of research that may be acceptable for them but are perhaps not useful and indeed may be quite harmful in our own field. The series of papers in this volume do not treat other possibilities at all. It is perhaps something that ought to be dealt with in another volume. We do feel that the consideration of alternative models of research as well as the development of entirely new ones is an issue that demands the attention of the most competent minds in the field.

What areas of reading research demand emphasis?

Linguistics and reading research

Reading is a broad field related to many other fields. The annual summary of investigations, which appears as a full issue of *Reading Research Quarterly* each year, regularly monitors journals in such diverse areas as neurology, sociology, learning disabilities, optometry, psychology, linguistics, child development, and fine arts, among others. It would be appropriate perhaps to include papers on the problems of conducting investigations in each of these areas as they relate to reading. Space limitations among other factors militated against this. The current productivity of and interest in research on linguistics and reading demanded that it be singled out and represented in this volume.

The importance of linguistics in gaining insights into the reading process cannot be disputed. The need to improve the quality of research efforts in this area is as great as in any other area. Goodman and Wardhaugh address themselves to the problems of conducting reading-linguistic research as each perceives these problems. Their approaches are from very different perspectives, and the reader gains by noting the differences in thinking.

On at least one point, both Goodman and Wardhaugh are in agreement; and they are joined by Wardrop, a statistician, in stressing the need to find appropriate tools for conducting research and in recognizing the dangers inherent in overreliance on statistically sophisticated designs.

Longitudinal efforts

Among the more promising general types of research is longitudinal. It is a type, rather than a specific design. Blake and Allen discuss various research designs appropriate for use in conducting longitudinal studies.

In the field of reading there exists a plethora of research of various kinds. That abundance does not exist when one attempts to identify longitudinal studies, which are scarce. If research tends to be a one-shot activity and much of that is dissertation research, part of the problem is explained. Doctoral students generally do not have the time to conduct longitudinal studies—at least not as doctoral programs tend to be set up now. No doubt many postdoctoral researchers feel the pressure of "publish or perish," and this pressure does not permit them the luxury of longitudinal research efforts.

We wonder if longitudinal research really is a luxury or whether it is a necessity. In so many other fields, the 5-minute data collection procedure that is so widely prevalent in our field would be viewed with the gravest alarm. If the individual collecting the brief sample of data baptizes them with a liberal sprinkling of holy water statistics, they tend to be accepted as blessed. If the statistical design dazzles enough, we forgive the fact that all sorts of conclusions are drawn on the basis of one poorly designed test administered to X number of children at one brief sitting. And all sorts of inappropriate implications are drawn from these data.

Appropriate longitudinal research can give us answers to questions of major significance and importance. Perhaps it is our *only* means to do so. The field of reading begs for carefully designed, well-executed longitudinal investigations, which have been heralded in other fields. They offer promise of breaking new grounds and developing new insights.

Interdisciplinary efforts

Because reading interfaces with so many other fields, it becomes important that we know what those other disciplines have to offer. It is, of course, impossible for most of us to know a number of fields in a scholarly sense. Increasingly, then, it would seem that interdisciplinary research efforts should be encouraged.

Such efforts date back a number of years and stand out prominently because of their relative sparseness in the literature. At least one such report, now over 30 years old, provides one model for interdisciplinary research. We refer to Robinson's *Why Pupils Fail in Reading* (1946). In this particular study, a reading person served as the coordinator and integrator for the overall research effort. If the focus is to be reading, as we would hope it would be, then the model is as valid and useful now as it was then.

Interdisciplinary efforts can provide us with more than just the insights offered by scholars in allied disciplines relative to their insights into reading and the reading process. Such efforts are to be encouraged because they may also open paths to new types of research approaches used in other disciplines. The interchange of ideas, the comparisons of reading as viewed from several outside disciplines, and the opportunity to tap knowledge bases that may be otherwise unavailable to us all make interdisciplinary efforts an important type of research for members of the reading field to pursue. Before it can be undertaken with any degree of success, however, we must learn to communicate with members of other professions.

Other problems

Many problems of conducting research are discussed in the various papers included in this volume. Some of those have already been discussed; others need some reference at this point.

Bligh makes specific references to the many measurement issues in reading research. Among those, he refers to the criterion tests used. As editors of the *Quarterly*, we have the opportunity to see scores of manuscripts each year. We are constantly amazed at the cavalier-like manner in which tests are treated. It is not unusual to find no references whatsoever to the reliability and validity of new or author-developed instruments. Even sadder is to find a whole study based on the administration of several tests, the scores of which are then correlated, factor analyzed, or treated in some statistical manner. The findings are then treated as truth without *any* question being raised by the author relative to the appropriateness or validity of the instruments used. The author assumes, and expects his audience to assume, that the scores of the tests are infallible and that the tests are assessments of truth. We in the field of reading have reached all sorts of conclusions and have made all sorts of decisions based on highly suspect instruments.

Once the data are collected and analyzed, the researcher must interpret the meaning of his findings. Harris presents a number of cautions for the consumer of research. His cautions are also applicable to the producer. If followed, they would result in a superior product.

Schools have been less than warm in their reception toward research and researchers—often for good reasons. The researcher has frequently neglected to recognize that he sometimes disrupts the classroom or school routine in collecting his all-important data. More than occasionally he does not take the time to inform school personnel why his project is worthwhile, but rather assumes that everyone will be as impressed and excited about it as he is. Anastasiow presents many practical, helpful suggestions for the investigator who intends pursuing research in the school situation. His caveats, if employed, can only smooth the way to a happier experience on the part of both researcher and school.

As Tone notes, a research report can have only limited effect until it is shared with an audience. The final step in the good research report is presenting it in an organized, concise, and clear manner. More than one paper has been rejected by RRQ advisory board members because the author was unable to present his ideas in an understandable manner. Good organization and writing are difficult to teach. The Tone paper, applied, should go a long way toward aiding the writer in presenting his ideas well.

This volume grew out of an observed need to improve research efforts in reading. We turned to members of our advisory board to write many of these papers because we felt they represented an expertise rarely found in one small group of individuals. It seemed best in a first effort to focus on the neophyte researcher. Often that individual is more open to receiving aid because he is aware that he needs it; his ego is not as involved as is that of the mature researcher.

All problems of producing better research cannot be solved in one volume. However, it is hoped that the papers in this volume do help some researchers—who might otherwise have turned out another badly designed and much flawed study—to produce a product of which both they and the profession can be proud.

REFERENCES

CHALL, JEANNE S. *Learning to read: the great debate*. New York: McGraw-Hill, 1967.
GRAY, WILLIAM S. Reading. In *Encyclopedia of research in education*. New York: Macmillan, 1950, 965-1005.
ROBINSON, HELEN M. *Why pupils fail in reading*. Chicago: University of Chicago Press, 1946.

Identifying and planning reading research

HELEN M. ROBINSON, Emeritus
University of Chicago

A potential reading researcher needs to be aware of a myriad of problems before he decides to undertake research in reading. Perhaps the major problem is to determine that there really is a field of reading quite apart from that of related disciplines. Unless the researcher views reading as a whole dynamic area, he is likely to study bits and pieces that may have little or no significance in furthering understanding of the reading field.

Since the early 1960s, various models of the reading process have been developed in an effort to show how the different parts of reading fit together. None of these models have been widely accepted as comprehensive; yet each attempts to show what is known and what needs to be learned, and especially how the parts may fit together. Without some overall view, research may be inconsequential.

Some reassurance that there is a field of reading research may be offered by the fact that during the past 50 years, 8,230 studies have been identified and summarized in the "Summaries of Investigations Relating to Reading" (Weintraub et al., 1974). The majority of the studies, regardless of their scope or quality, were done by persons who consider reading to be their major field of study.

Throughout this period, however, persons from other disciplines have approached the study of reading as though it were a special area of another discipline. For example, the linguist may reason that reading is a special type of language study; the psychologist may argue that learning to read is an application of principles of learning. The sociologist may rightly see reading as a reflection of social change and as an instrument for producing that change. The librarian may view reading as a means of continuing self-education and/or a way to sort out and establish human values. The fact that reading embraces all of these views, and many others, is important because, without such knowledge, many factors are overlooked in a single study. Therefore, the potential reading researcher should see the correlation of all related views in extending the body of knowledge which is uniquely reading. To the extent that it is possible to unite fragmented research from other disciplines and to bring it to bear on the study of reading, it becomes a discipline in its own right.

Identification of a research problem, therefore, may require background and understanding of related disciplines as well as of the field of reading. Such understandings may be even more essential in planning the research because of the procedures and techniques among which the researcher must choose. The wide choices that must be made in each stage of research lead to the "systematic inquiry for verified knowledge" (Wise, Nordberg, and Reitz, 1967) which is the goal of all reading research.

Identifying research problems

A consistent review of research, year after year, for about 40 years, has shown a broad gamut of topics reported. In preparing for this paper, a number of people were asked, indirectly, how they chose their topics. The most common reply was "because I am interested in it." This is an important reason for making a choice because without a deep and pervading interest, few studies are carried through the labored processes to completion. Interest, however, may have different origins and be of different levels of intensity. It may arise from a genuine curiosity to learn something which is not known. Interest may be generated externally by pressures, one of which is often called the *need to publish*. In this case the interest may be much less intense than in the case of curiosity.

Other researchers are those who produce doctoral dissertations. Doctoral students also vary greatly in the intensity of their interests in given topics. One student may be so much interested in a topic that he will spend excessive time to develop means for studying the problem. In contrast, another student may select a topic which can be easily studied with his major interest being in completing the dissertation.

While there is a great variety of reasons for choosing topics for research, the most common ones can be grouped into several categories. The categories vary from accidentally finding data that may produce a publishable study to using the questions generated by one study as topics for succeeding ones.

1. Seeing available data

In this category are the post hoc studies in which the researcher finds data which have not been processed or reported. In most instances, no advance plan has been made to collect the data. In selecting such a topic, the researcher should be aware of the problems he may face when his study is completed.

Examples of this type of choice of a topic can be found in comparative studies of reading achievement of schools, of classes, of methods of teaching, or of school or classroom organization. Reading achievement test data may be found for fourth grade pupils among whom some of the children were taught by method A and others by method B in first grade. If the researcher chooses to use such a topic, he must recognize the confounding factors that may have occurred during and since first grade which will reduce the validity of his study. He may not even be able to find out how the tests were given or scored or whether he can depend on them to have measured any desired changes. He must be prepared to doubt any of his findings and be uncertain of interpretations.

In contrast, data may be found which were carefully collected in a study for another purpose but could be analyzed equally well for a new purpose. If the researcher has access to all of the details of the first study and finds that they meet the needs for his prospective study, then he may anticipate results as dependable as those of the study for which the data were originally collected.

Topics for research chosen because data are found, without advance planning, are not plentiful and, therefore, the researcher should approach such a choice with great care.

2. Seeking practical answers

This category includes the identification of a topic which will help school personnel solve problems. This category differs from the preceding one in that the study may be planned in advance. In some instances, however, school administrators simply request evaluation of the effectiveness of certain plans and procedures. The researcher who chooses a topic in which all data except current evaluations are in retrospect must anticipate questionable results. For example, such factors as the types of pupils, the quality of instruction and enthusiasm of teachers, the amount of time given to reading instruction, and the facilities available may not have been recorded over the years of instruction.

The researcher who chooses to help school personnel solve problems of instruction may do so by insisting that the plans be made in advance and that adequate procedures be followed. Thus the researcher's topic is more likely to satisfy him, as well as help the particular school solve problems, without the bias and confounding effects often found in reports of research. The researcher who chooses topics of this type needs to be aware that the results may be limited to the school system with which he is dealing.

3. Searching for a problem

Many graduate students, as well as others, may search the literature for unsolved problems which appeal to them. There are common ways in which the literature is used to suggest topics to those who seek problems. First, the individual may read in an area of interest to him and locate one or several problems that he would like to study. Of course, he must make a thorough search of the existing literature on the topics to find out if these topics have been studied previously, what answers have been found, and whether there are still problems to be solved.

Second, some graduate students who have not had an adequate foundation in existing research look for sources of unsolved problems published by researchers from time to time (Durrell, 1936; Gray, 1952; Robinson, 1968, 1970).

Third, the person who has systematically covered the research of the 1900s should identify so many problems that need solution through research that a choice of the many topics may be difficult. In addition, one who has such a background will usually keep abreast of ongoing research reviewed annually in the *Reading Research Quarterly,* in the annual *Proceedings of the National Reading Conference,* and in *Elementary English.* The problems of choosing a topic for research are quite different for this person than for those who have had little contact with the literature and have limited familiarity with unsolved problems in reading because so many problems become evident that he may not be able to decide which one to choose.

4. Obtaining guidance

Doctoral students especially, but also some neophyte researchers, may ask established researchers for suggested topics. Sometimes they send a short questionnaire asking the mature researcher to suggest important topics; from the ideas secured, the students may select the most appealing ones. In addition, such a questionnaire may ask about topics which would be investigated if unlimited time were available to the established researcher. A variety of other questions may be included to provide leads to topics considered important.

The doctoral candidate must satisfy a major professor or advisor, and usually a committee, that his topic is significant. Professors vary markedly in their procedures in dealing with doctoral students in this respect. Some assign topics closely related to their own interests or to expand their own research. In contrast, other professors insist that students identify a topic in which they are interested, even though it may be totally unrelated to their professor's interest.

The doctoral seminar at some universities provides opportunities for those students seeking a topic for research to exchange ideas with others who are gathering data or have completed their studies. The advantages are numerous but two deserve mention. One is that the problems inherent in research on a given topic may become evident and either discourage or encourage the selection of topics likely to pose similar problems. A second advantage is that the beginner may see aspects of the problem which have not been studied, or extensions which need to be undertaken. Techniques for studying a particular problem may be seen as means of exploring a topic in which the beginner is already interested. The seminar may save time for graduate students wishing to identify a topic for research.

5. Enlisting in a cooperative project

In some instances two or more graduate or postgraduate students wish to select a single topic and carry on cooperative studies. When cooperative research is planned by a mature researcher and each student carries out one phase of the study, the student may complete his dissertation more quickly; but he should be aware of the experiences he is missing. Specifically, the student does not learn, under guidance, how to identify a problem and plan it himself.

However, cooperative research may be a valuable experience when two or more persons with differing backgrounds plan to attack a problem from different points of view. New insights may be extended while the education of those who cooperate is broadened. For example, a person with a major background in psychology or sociology who teams up with one whose background has been in teaching may broaden the research base of the topic they choose. Although persons from various disciplines plan together, each should be responsible for developing his own aspect of the study so that he may learn how to become an independent researcher.

Graduate students who have an opportunity to work as assistants to professors on their own studies may learn a great deal if they are able to participate in the early phases of choosing topics and planning research. In addition, after the professor's problem is delimited, numerous ancillary problems may be obvious so that they can serve as topics for study by students.

The Reading Research Center at the University of Chicago, with its multidisciplinary advisory committee, provided opportunities for graduate and postgraduate assistants to learn about identifying and plan-

Identifying and planning research

ning research. Under close supervision, beginners did routine tasks, such as giving and scoring tests, carrying out observations, and searching the literature on given topics. As students became more competent, they accepted greater responsibility. Postdoctoral research associates were able to codirect a study and/or develop one of their own. All staff members met to discuss problems as they arose, and the Advisory Committee brought the knowledge of several disciplines to bear on research problems of both the staff and the students.

Neophyte researchers who wish to have experience with mature researchers may become members of research and development centers; some of these are independent while others are located at universities.

An example of an earlier extensive cooperative project involved 27 centers (Bond, 1966) with numerous experienced and less mature researchers. First grade methods of teaching reading were being examined and, in most instances, the choice of topics was narrowed to two or three. Large cooperative studies of this type are rare, but they can be a source of training and experience, both in identifying topics and in planning and conducting research.

6. Continuing to study a topic

Those persons who use this technique for identifying research topics are limited in number. Problems in reading will never be solved by "one-shot" studies, as Barton and Wilder (1964) characterized them. While single studies of a given topic may be useful if they enter a new area, if they develop a promising technique for investigation, or even if they show that certain hypotheses are not tenable, single studies usually just scratch the surface. Indeed, most of them open up more problems than they solve. For example, a good doctoral dissertation should suggest enough research topics to launch a researcher on his major career if he continues to pursue these unsolved problems. Unfortunately, few people in reading follow one study after another on the same topic until some dependable answers are obtained. Perhaps this failure accounts for the characterization of reading research as fragmentary and of less value than it should be in view of the thousands of reports available.

There are tremendous advantages in continuing to investigate the same topic, if it is significant to the field. The researcher already has a background of previous investigations, has developed a rationale for the topic, and most important, has had first-hand experience in using promising techniques so that he recognizes limitations which he can plan to eliminate.

Another aspect of this category involves other persons continuing the investigations done by one researcher. As a result of an ongoing doctoral seminar at the University of Chicago in which each student reported on his research periodically up to the final oral examinations, a series of studies was done on visual and auditory perception. Later the writer combined the results of these studies and did a larger investigation than could be expected of any graduate student (Robinson, 1972).

In the past, most continuing studies have resulted from a new technique for investigation. No doubt many examples are familiar but two or three may be useful to neophytes. The development of the eye-movement camera and its improved successors sparked dozens of investigations of how the eye behaves during reading. Studies spanned the gamut of age from beginners to adults and of content from prose and poetry to pictures; and it probed behavior in a number of different languages as in the Unesco report (Gray, 1963). With refined methods of recording and computer counting, the technique is currently in use to determine time for processing input versus time for saccadic fixations (Abrams and Zuber, 1972). Along with the improvements in instrumentation has come greater sophistication in research design and improved statistical techniques to determine the dependability of the data secured.

A second example of continuing to use a technique is current. The cloze procedure was developed by Taylor (1954) and has been used by dozens of researchers with different populations and for different purposes (Rankin, 1965 and Jongsma, 1971). Concurrently, some researchers such as John Bormuth are continuously exploring the cloze procedure as a measure of readability and as a measure of comprehension; and they have related it to various linguistic units.

There are, then, many and varied ways used by prospective researchers to identify topics. Neophytes may need guidance while mature researchers usually have the next topic in mind before the preceding study is completed.

Choosing among topics

When the prospective researcher has found several or a multitude of problems begging for solution, he cannot proceed on all topics at one time so he must choose the one he will pursue first. This choice involves more than interest in a topic; it involves the competency of the researcher in different areas and available facilities to do the study. One way to examine the practical possibilities of conducting research on a given topic is to look at the major areas into which past research has been classified.

Since 1925 when Gray published his first summary, research in reading has been classified as the *sociology of reading, the physiology of reading, the psychology of reading,* and *the teaching of reading.* (See the Annual Summary of Research Relating to Reading in the *Reading Research Quarterly.*)

The *sociology of reading* includes topics dealing with how reading functions in individual and social life so that society can attain its goals and standards. It deals primarily with adults as subjects. One example of problems in this area is the extent of illiteracy and its relations to social problems, employment, national development and the like. Others are reading in relation to other mass media; readership of newspapers, magazines, and books; and reading interests of adults. Readability of adult materials and the effects of reading are further examples. Cultural and ethnic factors as they relate to reading in the social setting are problems of current concern.

Topics included in *physiology of reading* include the physical, neurological, and psychophysical factors involved in reading. Studies in this area have included such topics as endocrine balance, vision and hearing problems, neurological disorders, effects of dominant and recessive hemispheres of the brain, and electroencephalographic results. Psychophysical factors have included studies of the heart rate, respiration rate, and the like, especially in relation to what is read.

Examples of topics classified as the *psychology of reading* are experiments in learning to read, visual and auditory perception, language abilities basic to reading, personality and self-concept, and readability. Causes of reading disability or factors related to it cover both physical and psychological categories.

The teaching of reading includes topics dealing with methods of instruction and with materials, ranging from the earliest years to adulthood. Also studies considering treatment of reading disability are placed in this category.

Examination of research completed in these categories reveals that there are differences in methods of study, of instruments used, and of sampling—all of which may influence the selection of a topic for research. An example of a topic from each category should illustrate some important differences.

In the sociological area, a topic might be concerned with what adults read in the United States. Obviously it would be impossible to study all adults, so it is necessary to know how sampling procedures are developed and used, to have the procedures for securing information on what is read, and to have the background to interpret the data gathered.

In the area of psychology, a topic could relate to visual information processing. To make such a study might require an instrument as complicated as a cathode ray oscillograph controlled by a computer. Moreover, the stimuli would need to be designed to be appropriate to solve the problem. The age and reading competence of the subjects would influence findings, and the problem of securing a representative sample of subjects should be considered.

Topics dealing with the teaching of reading are sufficiently familiar so that illustrations are superfluous. Usually they are done in schools, although a few are carried out in laboratories. A thorough discussion of this type of research appears in the *Handbook of Research on Teaching* (1963).

In selecting a research topic, each individual should assess his own background to undertake the problem. For example, historical research, which is a survey of past events in reading related to the social setting of the particular period of time, can be done most readily by one who has competence in the general methods of historical research. Studies in the sociology of reading require an understanding of sociology and the research methods used by sociologists. Unless the researcher is willing to invest considerable time in developing a background in a particular discipline, he may wish to consider topics in which his background permits an understanding of research procedures and interpretation of results.

Neither identification nor selection of a research topic in reading is a simple process if an excellent study is anticipated. Many factors must be considered before the planning of the study begins.

Planning reading research

Planning research is the most important step of the entire study. It is time-consuming and, if properly done, may even discourage those not really committed to research.

For doctoral students, discriminative selection of a topic and careful advance planning pay large dividends in the quality of the final product and often reduce the casualties on the final oral examination.

A number of steps must be followed in preparing a carefully conceived plan for research. The most important ones are discussed briefly, but the order may be changed, depending on previous investigation of the topic and experience of the researcher.

Searching the literature

The previous literature search to identify a topic has usually uncovered a great many sources and studies which were read for that purpose. At this point, it is essential to do careful *documentary research*, which is analysis of *what* has been done and *how* it was accomplished in relation to a specific topic. This survey should be extensive and the analysis should be critical. In other words, all studies related to the chosen topic should be evaluated to determine their strengths and weaknesses and their contributions to the solution of the problems.

A half dozen or more checklists may be found to guide the evaluation of previous research, but guided practice appears to be the best means for acquiring the ability to read research critically. As the studies are examined, time is saved if full references and notes are made for each one. Some of these references will be needed later in developing the rationale and providing the theoretical framework for the report.

When the literature search has been completed, it is possible to determine the aspects of the chosen topic which have been successfully studied and those in need of further research. In addition, the methods for research can be reviewed to ascertain the ones which were most productive and those which were least satisfactory. It is always possible that newer techniques of investigation or of data treatment have developed and are applicable too.

Delimiting the problems

Doctoral candidates and inexperienced researchers often need guidance in delimiting their problems to manageable size because they tend to seek answers to too many questions in one study. On the other hand, the problems must not be so limited as to be trivial. If a list of unanswered questions is made during the literature search, it is possible to choose the most significant or pervasive ones to pursue. Often several questions can be combined into one that throws light on answers to the others. Sometimes it is essential to consider several components of a problem because each influences the other.

Developing hypotheses

In planning research, one of the essential steps is to state the hypotheses to be tested. Surprisingly, even some so-called experimental studies contain no stated hypotheses, and often no clearly stated questions. Such studies may be compared to a "fishing trip" in which one is satisfied with any fish that bites the bait. Hypotheses usually state the expectations of the researcher, *if* the anticipated procedures are followed. The exception is the null hypotheses, stated primarily to satisfy statistical criteria.

The researcher must be certain that the hypotheses are stated in a form that is testable. For example, if a hypothesis states that an experimental group will read *better* than a control group after a given treatment, what is meant? The words *read better* may imply oral reading, silent reading, or a higher quality of materials read. And how much is better—a point or two on a test, or a statistically significant difference favoring the experimental group? In other words, the hypotheses must be stated so that they can be confirmed or rejected.

Another problem in stating hypotheses is the implication of cause-and-effect when the question is really whether two changes occur together.

The clarity and objectivity of the statement of hypotheses guide the procedures the researcher plans to follow. Hypotheses suggest to the researcher the data which will be relevant and enable him to reject the collection of irrelevant data. In addition, hypotheses project the framework for conclusions to be reached when the study is completed.

Finally, the number of hypotheses generated may show the researcher that his study is too broad and not manageable. In turn, he may redefine his problem, leaving less important hypotheses for another study if necessary. Also, it is possible that the problem has been defined in such a way that no hypotheses can be tested by known means. In this case, refinement of the topic may be in order.

Estimating projected research time

When the hypotheses are clearly written, the researcher can estimate the time that will be needed to do the study. Usually even the experienced researcher underestimates the time required to complete a study because so many unforeseen problems arise. However, the neophyte often has no basis for estimate and, therefore, plans his research entirely unrealistically.

Two aspects of the time problem should be estimated. One relates to the number of man-days expected to be available for the study and whether they will be available when they are needed most. For example, a study of certain characteristics of beginners in school may require a great deal of time at the start of the school year. If time is not available *then,* changes in pupils will occur before they are studied.

A second important aspect of time is the number of years anticipated to test the hypotheses. For example, some investigations of the teaching of reading must be extended several years to determine whether advantages or disadvantages to a treatment are temporary or permanent.

A disproportionate or unreasonable amount of time doing a doctoral dissertation can be frustrating, lead to dropouts, and discourage future research. On the other hand, a limited amount of time should never take precedence over the selection of a significant topic. Sometimes ancillary data can readily be obtained to provide a base for a second study after the dissertation, but a realistic assessment of time needed for research should be stressed by every advisor of doctoral candidates.

Acquiring special competencies

In planning research, it is important to assess the special competencies that will be required to test the hypotheses. Understandings in such areas should be developed before the study is begun rather than at various points during the investigation. Experimental studies require competence in measurement or assessment and knowledge of statistical analysis of data. These competencies would be acquired before planning the study because, as Wise, Nordberg, and Reitz (1967) said, "Elaborate statistics cannot substitute for basic misconceptions, or for failures of experimental control . . . ."

Statistics is an area in which many doctoral candidates need to develop competence. They expect to gather data and compare the findings. As Guba (1963) has explained, statistical procedures are not a research plan but a tool to provide inferential conclusions from proper samples of subjects. However, statistical procedures have developed so rapidly with the advent of computers that it is usually helpful to consult a statistician, no matter how well-prepared the researcher is in the field. Consultation should occur during the planning stage to avoid errors that cannot be corrected after the data are gathered. The researcher who is competent in statistics can be sure that the guidance given helps him plan to test his hypotheses rather than to do a major statistical study.

Competence in measuring or assessing reading characteristics to be studied by standardized tests may be acquired from a critical review of similar investigations, from reliable sources such as Buros' *Mental Measurements Yearbook* or from recent books about measurement in reading such as that by Farr (1969). However, many hypotheses are tested more precisely by means other than standardized tests. For example, in a study of first graders' attitudes toward reading when i.t.a. was used, an attitude test had to be devised, tried out, revised, and finally used. Logs of time spent in teaching may be needed. Observation schedules which permit a high degree of agreement among observers may have to be devised. A questionnaire or structured interview requires the same care in preparation as any other instrument for a study.

In addition to measurement or assessment of reading, it may be essential to become familiar with ways to determine factors which confound the experimental data. Many of these factors are not determinable by standardized tests.

Securing sources of data

Different kinds of sources are essential to different types of studies. For example, historical research is based on original documents. Comparative research can be done only if subjects with different characteristics are available to compare.

Experimental research in reading usually is done with children but sometimes with adult subjects. In planning research, therefore, the hypotheses should guide the investigator to a specification of the characteristics of the subjects needed: age or grade level; good, average, or poor readers or an unselected group; high or low socioeconomic levels.

Schools are the major source of subjects, so the researcher should identify schools enrolling children appropriate for collecting data. Then it is essential to obtain cooperation from the schools. Usually permission comes from administrators, but sometimes from school boards and parents too. Teachers are extremely important in cooperative efforts in research. If children are to come to a laboratory, more detailed permissions and cautions are needed than if they are to be studied in the school setting. It is wise to secure written agreements between the researcher and the schools.

If appropriate subjects cannot be obtained, the problem may need to be altered or even abandoned temporarily. Unselected groups of adult subjects are even more difficult to obtain; college students are frequently used but they represent a selected group.

If a study is planned to require a short period of time, the rate of turnover of subjects is not so crucial as when the study is planned to use the same subjects for several years. In the latter case, a search should be made for schools with stable populations or school systems willing to permit researchers to follow subjects, at least those who transfer within the system. Even so, one should plan to include alternate subjects to avoid excessive potential losses from year to year.

Doing pilot studies

One way to ascertain the level of cooperation of a school system or a particular school is to carry on a ministudy. For example, the writer selected an innercity school that made every adjustment needed to gather data easily. At the same time, a suburban school, known for its interest in research, required a year of preparation before the experiment could begin. The pilot study permitted the researcher to check the adequacy of random assignment to classes before school opened, enabled the researcher to meet with parent groups in advance, and assured smooth operation of testing and observation early the following school year.

Pilot studies serve other purposes and one or several may be needed. They help the experimenter refine his techniques for investigation, try out his data-collection schedule, and get acquainted with the teachers so they do not feel apart from the experiment.

In unexplored areas, a number of pilot studies may be needed. For example, Piekarz (1954) carried on a dozen or so pilot studies to identify the best selections for her purpose, and to find the most productive sectioning of the selections so that the greatest amount of verbalization about retrospective thinking could be obtained.

Pilot studies often lead the researcher back to refinement of his hypotheses and/or plans for data gathering which result in improvement in the main experiment.

A pilot study should never be confused with a major study. Seldom are these tryout studies publishable unless the techniques used in them might save the time of other researchers.

Writing the plan

Each research plan should be written, even in its earliest and crudest form. As a rule, each plan needs to be revised and sharpened many times during the period of planning. When it is in final form, the written plan commits the researcher to each step of his procedure up to the completion of the study.

As the plan is written, the researcher should be especially alert to any assumptions he has made and, wherever possible, the number should be reduced. It is unwise to make an assumption if there is a way to avoid it.

In planning research, a few limitations may be unavoidable, but notations should be made in the plan. Further limitations usually appear during the course of data collection. The prospective researcher needs to ask, in advance, whether there are too many limitations to interpret any findings with confidence. Then he can alter his plan or approach the problem from another vantage point if necessary.

The final part of the plan is speculation on the various alternatives that could result from the findings. For example, if one hypothesis is supported and a second one rejected, the researcher should anticipate how this could occur and what could account for it. By examining the meanings of the possible outcomes, the researcher is anticipating relationships among the hypotheses, that is, he is reasoning about whether each supports or refutes the others as they are written. The projection of alternative outcomes may lead him back to reexamine his hypotheses or it may suggest that he is prepared for any results that are found.

The carefully chosen topic which is planned in accordance with accepted and thoughtful procedures is likely to make the greatest contribution to knowledge about reading. Improved research planning can contribute immeasurably to the quality of reading research.

REFERENCES

ABRAMS, S. G., & ZUBER, B. L. Some temporal characteristics of information processing during reading. *Reading Research Quarterly,* Fall 1972, *8*, 40-51.
BARTON, ALLEN H., & WILDER, DAVID E. Research and practice in the teaching of reading: a progress report. In Matthew B. Miles (Ed.), *Innovations in education.* New York: Teachers College, Columbia University, 1964.
BUROS, OSCAR K. (Ed.) *Mental measurements yearbook.* Highland Park, New Jersey: Gryphon Press, 1938 and intermittently thereafter.
CAMPBELL, DONALD T., & STANLEY, JULIAN C. Experimental and quasi-experimental designs for research on teaching. In N. L. Cage (Ed.), *Handbook of research on teaching.* Chicago: Rand McNally, 1963. Pp. 171-246.
DURRELL, DONALD D. Research problems in the elementary schools. *Elementary English Review,* April 1936, *13*, 149-156 and May 1936, *13*, 184-192.

FARR, ROGER. *Reading: what can be measured?* Newark, Delaware: International Reading Association, 1969.

GRAY, WILLIAM S. Needed research in reading. *Elementary English,* February 1952, *29,* 100-109.

GRAY, WILLIAM S. *The teaching of reading and writing.* Paris: Unesco, 1963. (Distributed by Scott, Foresman, Glenview, Illinois)

GRAY, WILLIAM S. Summary of investigations relating to reading. *Supplementary educational monographs,* No. 28. Chicago: University of Chicago Press, 1925.

GUBA, EGON G. Common sense about experimental design in educational research. Unpublished paper read at a Faculty Symposium, School of Education, New York University, February 25, 1963.

JONGSMA, EUGENE. *The cloze procedure as a teaching technique.* Newark, Delaware: International Reading Association, 1971.

PIEKARZ, JOSEPHINE. Individual differences in interpretation. Unpublished doctoral dissertation, University of Chicago, 1954.

RANKIN, EARL F. Cloze procedure: a survey of research. *Yearbook of the South West Reading Conference,* 1965, *14,* 133-148.

ROBINSON, HELEN M. The next decade. In Helen M. Robinson (Ed.), *Innovation and change in reading instruction.* Sixty-Seventh Yearbook of the National Society for the Study of Education, Part II. Chicago: University of Chicago Press, 1968. Pp. 400-420.

ROBINSON, HELEN M. Significant unsolved problems in reading. *Journal of Reading,* November 1970, *14,* 77-82 and 134-141.

ROBINSON, HELEN M. Visual and auditory modalities related to methods for beginning reading, *Reading Research Quarterly,* 8, Fall 1972, 7-41.

TAYLOR, WILSON L. Cloze procedure: a new tool for measuring readability, *Journalism Quarterly, 30,* Fall 1953.

WEINTRAUB, SAMUEL; ROBINSON, HELEN M.; SMITH, HELEN K.; PLESSAS, GUS; & ROWLS, MICHAEL. Summary of investigations relating to reading, July 1, 1973 to June 30, 1974. *Reading Research Quarterly, 10,* 3, entire issue.

WISE, JOHN E.;NORBERG, ROBERT B.; & REITZ, DONALD J. *Methods of research in education.* Boston: D. C. Heath, 1967.

Design problems in reading research

JAMES L. WARDROP
University of Illinois at Urbana-Champaign

It is not easy to do meaningful research. It is no easier in reading than in any other field. First of all, good research depends on asking good questions. In this discussion of research design, it is assumed that you already have a good question without even worrying about what criteria are applied to decide the "goodness" of the question.

Most good questions deal with one or more of perhaps four major categories related to the reading process: theoretical formulations, instructional techniques, learner skills, and what might be called "measurement research." For example, research related to theoretical formulations focuses on such orientations as psycholinguistics or information processing; research on instructional techniques might consider a phonics approach, the *Distar* program, or some other special training program; research on learner skills emphasizes such issues as one versus several "ability factors," the relationship of reading to listening skills, or differences among various subgroups of learners (so-called "disabled readers" are a popular subgroup for research); and measurement research deals with such issues as how to measure comprehension or problems in diagnostic assessment.

Superimpose on this categorization a distinction between *exploratory* and *confirmatory* research. In the former, one adopts a stance of "ignorance" about some phenomenon and designs a study which will hopefully reduce the level of ignorance and even suggest questions for further study in confirmatory research. Confirmatory research involves the formulation of specific hypotheses (informed guesses, predictions) about a phenomenon, followed by the design of a study which seeks to confirm—or disconfirm—the guesses.

A crucial component in the development of a research design is a clear and logical justification for the predictions one makes. This is probably the most neglected aspect of the research process. We are prone to proceed as if our hypotheses have sprung full-bloom and are so obvious as to need no justification. Again, in this discussion it is assumed that you have clearly justified the hypotheses you are to test although much of what follows is related to this issue.

In reading research, the predominant modes of inquiry require the collection of information, usually quantitative information. The collecting of such information is usually mediated by various tests, questionnaires, or observation instruments. Many an otherwise worthwhile research study has foundered on measurement inadequacies. Indeed, the measurement problems may be the most important limitation to "good" reading research. Since these problems are discussed by Bligh elsewhere in this volume, they are not treated here.

Having ruled out question asking, hypothesis justification, and measurement problems, what is left for us to consider? What is left is the problem of developing a research design, which in fact answers the question or questions asked. A good research design is one which accomplishes two major purposes: it allows us to rule out alternative explanations for the phenomena we observe, and it leads to minimizing errors—both inferential and statistical.

Research design to rule out alternative explanations[1]

One of the best guides to doing "good" research is a 1964 article by John Platt in *Science* magazine, "Strong Inference." Although it was written from a physical-science perspective, it seems especially relevant for educational researchers. A systematic application of the philosophy articulated by Platt would yield more significant advances in our understanding of reading in the next decade than in the last half century. That is a strong statement—especially when it turns out that what Platt advocates is essentially what we have all been taught to call "the" scientific method. But let me paraphrase parts of Platt's article before you pass judgment. He asks:

> Why should there be . . . rapid advance in some fields and not in others? I think the usual explanations that we tend to think of—such as the tractability of the subject, or the quality or education of [those]

---

[1] Two extremely useful references here are Campbell and Stanley's monograph (1966) on *Experimental and Quasi-Experimental Designs* and a book by David Cox (1958), *Planning of Experiments*. Taken together, these sources provide invaluable guidance for the researcher.

drawn into it, or the size of research contracts—are important but inadequate. I have begun to believe that the primary factor in scientific advance is an intellectual one. These rapidly moving fields are fields where a particular method of doing . . . research is systematically used and taught, an accumulative method of inductive inference that is so effective that I think it should be given the name of "strong inference" [p. 347].

. . .

Strong inference consists of applying the following steps to every [research] problem . . . , formally and explicitly and regularly:
1. Devising *alternative* hypotheses;
2. Devising a crucial experiment (or several of them), with *alternative possible outcomes,* each of which will, as nearly as possible, exclude one or more of the hypotheses;
3. Carrying out the experiment so as to get a clear result;
4. Recycling the procedure, making subhypotheses or sequential hypotheses to refine the possibilities that remain; and so on.

It is like climbing a tree. At the first fork, we choose—or, in this case, "nature" or the experimental outcome chooses—to go to the right branch or the left; at the next branch, to go left or right; and so on . . . .

On any new problem, of course, inductive inference is not as simple and certain as deduction, because it involves reaching out into the unknown. Steps 1 and 2 [devising hypotheses and experiments] require intellectual inventions, which must be cleverly chosen so that hypothesis, experiment, outcome, and exclusion will be related in a rigorous syllogism . . . . What the formal schema reminds us to do is to try to make these inventions, to take the next step, to proceed to the next fork, without dawdling or getting tied up in irrelevancies [pp. 347-348].

. . .

The strong-inference attitude is evident just in the style and language in which the papers are written [p. 348].

Such papers are characterized by the inclusion of such statements as "Our conclusions . . . might be invalid if . . . (i) . . . (ii) . . . or (iii) . . . [is true]. We shall describe experiments which eliminate these alternatives." Or, in a discussion of competing theoretical explanations, we find a list of propositions derived from those theories which are "subject to denial"; the author also suggests which ones would be "most vulnerable to experimental test."

Such a research attitude is almost the inverse of the kind of thinking which characterizes most reading research. Such theories as we have involve intensely personal belief systems. Instead of looking for evidence to contradict (and thereby deny or exclude) a theory, we are prone to develop strong ego involvement in a theory and to seek to assimilate evidence supporting it, sometimes even refusing to acknowledge openly contradictory evidence. Or, we have a pet theory and wish to demolish its competitors. We encounter considerable difficulty when we try to apply a strong-inference approach to a field such as reading. We seem to be faced with a choice between being softheaded, as has typically been the case, or disputatious. The hang-up is our tendency to identify theories with individuals and—more crucially—to identify individuals with theories. Thus, to challenge a theory (or a hypothesis) is often tantamount to challenging the professional competence of a colleague. Platt suggests a way out of the dilemma—a method attributed to a geologist named Chamberlin:

> "To avoid this grave danger, the method of multiple working hypotheses is urged. It differs from the simple working hypothesis in that it distributes the [researcher's] effort and divides the affections. . . . Each hypothesis suggests its own criteria, its own means of proof, its own method of developing the truth, and if a group of hypotheses encompass the subject on all sides, the total outcome of means and of methods is full and rich" [p. 350].

Platt continues:

> . . . whenever each man begins to have multiple working hypotheses, it becomes purely a conflict between ideas. It becomes much easier then for each of us to aim every day at conclusive disproofs—at strong inference—without either reluctance or combativeness . . . [p. 350].

> In considering the effectiveness of research, Platt notes that:

> . . . the evident effectiveness of the systematic use of strong inference suddenly gives us a yardstick for thinking about the effectiveness of [research] methods in general. Surveys, taxonomies . . . , systematic measurements and tables, theoretical computations—all have their proper and honored place, provided they are parts of a chain of precise induction of how nature works . . . [p. 351].

> . . .

> We speak piously of taking measurements and making small studies that will "add another brick to the temple of science." Most such bricks just lie around the brickyard [p. 351].

One last bit of advice from Platt provides us with a guide to learning to apply strong inference to both planning our own research and evaluating another's:

> It consists of asking in your own mind, on hearing any scientific explanation or theory put forward, "But sir, what experiment could disprove your hypothesis?"; or, on hearing . . . [an] experiment described, "But sir, what hypothesis does your experiment disprove?"

This goes straight to the heart of the matter. It forces everyone to refocus on the central question of whether there is or is not a testable scientific step forward [p. 351].

Very little by way of "how to" advice is being offered here. Questions like "How can I design a study which allows me to control for (x) while looking at the *effect* of (y) on (z)?" or "How can I look at the *relationship* between (y) and (z) independently of (x)?" are probably what most would-be researchers would like to see treated. But we must invariably answer the "how can I" questions by saying, "It depends." There *are* some general strategies to apply to such questions, but the "best" answer is not always the same. It would be pointless to try to present in a brief discussion the wealth of detailed information needed to develop a research design. Once you have formulated your question(s) and hypotheses *very precisely* (and they will probably still be too vague), then it is time to talk about whether covariance or randomized blocks or matched groups or pretest-posttest or some other approach fits best; about how to control for order-of-presentation effects; about "how large a sample" should be utilized (which really means "How small a sample can I get by with?"); and about all the other design issues that we need to consider when planning a research study. The examples just used all relate to the internal validity of an experiment. the extent to which we have eliminated potential sources of bias. Another set of questions has to do with external validity, the extent to which results from an experiment can be generalized.

Research design to minimize errors of inference

"How far can I generalize my results?" is one of the most frequent concerns of a researcher. The "proper" answer is disheartening: to only that population whose members had a chance to be included in the sample from which you obtained your data, and only under the same conditions. In most reading research such an answer drastically limits external validity (the term used by Campbell and Stanley in discussing issues related to generalizability). Most reading research—indeed, most social-science research—deals with what have been called "grab groups." That is, we study students in a single classroom or school or district—or maybe even two or three districts—or we expand our horizons to the level of a "statewide" study; but always our sampling procedures are guided more by convenience, accessibility, and economy than by principles of research methodology. Such constraints are, of course, unavoidable, so in the strictest interpretation of "generalization" we are effectively stymied. In the face of such a problem, we resort to what might be called—to contrast it with Platt's "strong inference"—"weak generalization." The approach is best described in a 1968 article by Bracht and Glass, "The External

Validity of Experiments." Essentially, the argument is a nonscientific one: we are willing to accept the notion that our particular sample is "like" some larger population with respect to those characteristics which we think might affect the experimental outcomes. Thus, even though practical considerations led us to use a "grab group," we are reasonably confident that we would obtain similar results with other groups from this larger population. It is on this basis that we cautiously generalize our results to a larger population than that from which we actually sampled. Needless to say, such generalizations cry out for replicating our research, each successful replication increasing our confidence in the validity of our generalizations. As an analogy in the physical sciences, consider the search for new chemical elements. A claim from one laboratory that a new element has been identified will not be accepted until another team of researchers at another location has used the same procedures and obtained the same result. For example, in 1926 element 61 in the periodic table had not been identified. That year, two University of Illinois chemists announced they had found it in ores containing elements 60 and 62. The same year a pair of Italian chemists at the University of Florence thought they had isolated the same element. But other chemists could not confirm the work of either group. It was not until 1945 that element 61, promethium, was isolated among the products of the fission of uranium. Only then were other scientists able to replicate the work of three chemists at Oak Ridge National Laboratory. Such demands for replicability are virtually unknown in the behavioral sciences.

There are some very real dangers in a weak generalization approach. We invariably pay for our soft-headedness. In this case, the hang-up is the assumption that the target population (to which we wish to generalize) does not differ from the experimentally accessible population (from which we obtained our sample) with respect to "those characteristics which . . . might affect the experimental outcomes." In the first place, we are *assuming*—often with good reason—that the target population is like the accessible population on the variables we consider relevant. More critically, we assume that we indeed know what the relevant variables are. Such an assumption is probably unwarranted in most reading research.

Research design to minimize experimental error

In conducting any research, we are always seeking precision. In other words, we always want to obtain the most accurate estimates we possibly can of the parameters of interest. It is about this function of research design that we are most often concerned since most of us are prone to think about research design primarily as it relates to statistical analysis.

Since it is impossible to deal adequately with this aspect of design in a reasonable amount of space, this paper addresses just a few general guidelines which help to minimize the hassles involved in doing "good" research.

Guideline 1: Keep it simple

Just because elaborate designs involving many factors—Latin squares, split-plots, and incomplete blocks—have worked well in some fields (notably, agriculture) does not mean that such designs are most appropriate for everyone. A common fault of doctoral students planning a dissertation (and some of us never outgrow it) is to equate good research with complex designs and elaborate statistical analysis.

Guideline 2: Let the question determine the method

This follows directly from the last comment. It may be because of the way statistics courses are taught, but doctoral students seem to choose an analysis technique first and then seek to formulate a question to fit the procedure.

Guideline 3: Avoid raw empiricism

Raw empiricism only clutters up the brickyard. Another isolated bit of data about a trivial question wastes time and talent. If it is true that people read to obtain meaning and that the purpose of instruction in reading is to enable the learner to obtain meaning, research in reading should be oriented toward understanding how meaning is acquired from printed symbols, after which we can deal with the instructional technology issues with something stronger than an ad hoc approach. The more common research style seems to be to accept some particular view of how meaning is acquired and to focus the research on questions about the effectiveness of various procedures for teaching reading in a manner consistent with that view. About such research, we should ask a form of one of Platt's questions, "But sir, what [important] hypothesis does [could] your experiment disprove?"

Guideline 4: Avoid empty theorizing

A theory without empirical support is of little value. More to the point, Platt notes that "A theory is not a theory unless it can be disproved. That is, unless it can be falsified by some possible experimental outcome." A theory which can account for every possible outcome is empty, worthless. A theory which does not lead to predictions subject to empirical disproof is merely an idle exercise. Ask Platt's other question: "But sir, what experiment could disprove your hypothesis?" If you can find a substantive answer to this question, you have the basis for your next important research study.

Guidelines 3 and 4 advise us to avoid both raw empiricism and empty theorizing. Taken together, they emphasize the necessity for a continuing interplay between theory and data. Without such interplay, research becomes sterile and lifeless; with such interplay, it is a lively and exciting experience.

Guideline 5: Maximize external validity

Reading researchers should be even more conscious than other social-science researchers that the phenomena to be studied relate to the functioning of real people in real-life settings. Although studies in rather artificial laboratory settings play a role in contributing to our understanding of the reading process, it is not until our theories and methods have been subjected to the test of general application in the classroom and elsewhere that we accept them. One of the external-validity problems not given sufficient attention is what Egon Brunswik called "ecological validity." In brief, if we seek theories and procedures to use in natural settings, we must ultimately turn to those natural settings for validating our theories and procedures.

Guideline 6: Maximize internal validity

Campbell and Stanley use "internal validity" to describe that aspect of experimental design which leads to the elimination of alternative explanations for empirical phenomena. In other words, design experiments in such a way that the only apparent explanation for positive outcomes is that which was hypothesized initially. In maximizing internal validity, we are guarding against the possibility that influences such as maturation, selection, and regression toward the mean might account for our results.

Guidelines 5 and 6 highlight the inescapable conflict between internal and external validity. Standard approaches to experimental design almost demand laboratory-like settings. Controlling extraneous influences, minimizing experimental error, ruling out alternative hypotheses—these ends cannot be easily achieved except in laboratory settings. Considerations of generalizability of findings from research involving human behavior demand ecological validity, field tests under natural, uncontrolled conditions.

Just where the balance should be struck between internal and external validity will vary from one study to the next. Sometimes the importance of laboratory control outweighs concerns about generalizability; at other times, generalizability is the overriding concern. Finding an optimal compromise between these conflicting demands is the essence of good research design.

Design problems

Considerations of nonexperimental research

To this point, this presentation has focused almost exclusively on experimentation, in which one controls one set of variables and looks at the effects of another set of variables on some observable outcome. There is another large class of studies which should be dealt with, studies in which we examine relationships among variables in the absence of direct experimental manipulation.

Although we tend to equate experimentation with one set of statistical-analysis procedures (exemplified by analysis-of-variance techniques) and associational studies with another set of analytic techniques (typically correlational), there is no necessary correspondence between statistical technique and type of study. Correlational techniques are sometimes used in experimental studies, and so-called inferential statistics are sometimes used to analyze associational data. Indeed, we have come to realize in recent years that both sets of analytical tools are specializations of the general linear model, and the essential equivalence of correlational and inferential approaches (to use the traditional labels) is now generally accepted.

Two examples of nonexperimental approaches to research illustrate the role and importance of research design in such studies. One actively debated issue among reading researchers continues to be the question of whether reading is a unitary skill or whether it involves the integration of a number of component skills. The common approach to this problem is to administer a set of measures of hypothesized component skills to a group and then submit the resulting scores to a factor analysis. Sounds straightforward enough, does it not? Unfortunately, manuscripts reporting such investigations almost never merit publication.

Why not? Let me suggest a few criteria to be applied to any study of this sort. Almost every manuscript fails to meet more than one of these criteria.

First, the investigator's choice of tests to measure the hypothesized skills is critical. Often the available standardized tests are rejected as measuring inappropriate skills or (presumably) having a factorially complex structure which would not facilitate the identification of such unitary skills as might exist. The investigator then constructs tests specifically for the study. When this happens, one must look for evidence of content and construct validity (including evidence that the items within a subtest are more like one another than they are like items in other subtests). Evidence for internal-consistency reliability is also essential. On the other hand, the researcher may choose to use subtests from available standardized test batteries. In this case, one looks for a clear and convincing rationale for the use of the chosen tests, a rationale which demonstrates the *possibility* that the hypothesized skills will in fact be measured. Simply put, the point is that the results of a factor analysis are critically dependent on the quality of the input data.

A second criterion relates to the number of different tests used to represent each hypothesized skill. It is necessary to realize that tests are grouped together in factor analysis on the basis of their statistical commonalities. In other words, if one has two tests of verbal aptitude and two others measuring finger dexterity, the verbal tests will be grouped together as one factor, while the performance measures will form a second factor. Now, if one has a test of reading comprehension, a test of verbal aptitude, a test of English usage, and a mathematics reasoning test (which typically has considerable verbal content), applying a factor analysis to the resulting scores is likely to yield a single "general" factor of verbal facility. Although the examples used to emphasize the point are extreme, the conclusion is equally true when designing similar studies to identify the skills involved in reading; namely, the study must include at least two—and preferably more—different measures of each hypothesized factor.

A third criterion requires that a sufficiently large number of subjects be tested. To operationalize "sufficiently large," let me state that there should be at least three times as many subjects tested as there are tests given. If fewer subjects are used, there seem to be some constraints on the test intercorrelations that make any factor-analytic results questionable.

A fourth criterion also relates to subjects. One must look for some evidence that they are from a clearly defined population in which there is reason to believe that there is variability among persons with respect to the skills being measured. After all, what we are trying to do is infer something about the structure of skills underlying the reading process for some population; and since factor analysis is based on correlational data, we need variability among the subjects in order to obtain meaningful correlations to work with.

Let us consider another approach to nonexperimental research, the search for causal relationships in the absence of experimentally manipulated variables. Sociologists and economists have been particularly innovative in exploring this area. In particular, the technique known as path analysis has had considerable utility in identifying causal patterns among sets of variables. In this approach, one hypothesizes a set of causal relationships among variables and derives a series of predictions about relationships which should be obtained among the variables if the model is appropriate. Those predictions are then tested by examining the correlations, regression weights, partial correlations, and/or partial regression weights actually obtained. Proper use of such approaches (and path analysis is only one of the several techniques available) requires Chamberlin's multiple working hypotheses. A researcher does not consider just one possible model; he considers alternative models and seeks to determine which one gives the closest match to the data. If you are interested in pursuing this topic, you will want to look at Maurice Tatsuoka's discussion in the first *Review of Research in Education* and Herbert Blaylock's book, *Causal Models in the Social Sciences*.

The two examples just given (a factor-analytic study and the search for causal models) are meant to illustrate the need for as much attention to research design in nonexperimental as in experimental research. The value of a strong-inference orientation and the importance of multiple working hypotheses apply equally for both kinds of research.

Final remarks

As the preceding discussion was meant to suggest, some research strategies offer more promise than others. Good research requires that we begin asking good questions. The need to challenge theories and hypotheses and continually seek to *dis*prove them is essential. Experimental research generally offers more promise for improving our understanding of reading than does nonexperimental. Finally, whether one is doing an experimental study or a nonexperimental one, the importance of attention to research design should not be underemphasized.

If reading research were guided by Platt's questions ("What experiment could disprove your hypothesis?" and "What hypothesis does your experiment disprove?"), if researchers were to adopt Chamberlin's notion of multiple working hypotheses, if designs were developed to maximize internal and external validity, advances in our understanding of the reading process would surely be astounding.

REFERENCES

BLAYLOCK, HUBERT M. *Causal models in the social sciences.* Chicago: Aldine-Atherton, 1971.
BRACHT, GLENN H., & GLASS, G. V. The external validity of experiments. *American Educational Research Journal,* 1968, *5,* 437-474.
CAMPBELL, DONALD T., & STANLEY, JULIAN C. *Experimental and quasi-experimental designs for research.* Chicago: Rand-McNally, 1966.
COX, DAVID R. *Planning of experiments.* New York: Wiley, 1958.
PLATT, JOHN R. Strong inference. *Science,* 1964, *146,* 347-352.
TATSUOKA, MAURICE M. Multivariate analysis in educational research. In Fred N. Kerlinger (Ed.), *Review of research in education,* Vol. 1. Itasca, Illinois: Peacock, 1973.

Measurement issues in reading research

HAROLD F. BLIGH
Harcourt Brace Jovanovich

The nationwide focus on reading has given rise to healthy questioning of current instructional methods and materials and to a search for guidelines to improve learning strategies. When reading research studies are carefully formulated, they provide valuable information for the kinds of decisions that need to be made. However, in designing and implementing a reading study, the researcher must be alert to measurement issues which unresolved can lead to inconclusive findings. The purpose of this paper is to call attention to the kinds of measurement problems that may arise and to offer some practical suggestions for dealing with them.

To do good research, we must first realize that a problem exists—a problem that is worthy of the time and effort to be spent in studying it. At least, the problem should merit seeking out information that will contribute to a better understanding of its ramifications. To adequately identify and describe a reading research problem, we must know how to ask good questions.

Among areas to investigate are those involving theoretical formulations, model development, instructional strategies, learner characteristics, and instrument development and validation. Some questions to ask are: What new theories of learning are emerging? Can reading theory be applied in the classroom? How do children learn to read? Do all children follow the same behavioral patterns in learning to read?

In attempting to answer such questions through planned research, we usually become involved in collecting information, quantifying and analyzing data, and drawing interpretations and making generalizations.

Relevant information may be obtained through talking with reading experts and searching the literature, by carrying out carefully planned experimental studies, and by administering tests and making other kinds of controlled observations. Dr. Wardrop's article develops six guidelines for conducting good reading research. He emphasizes the asking of meaningful questions and the development of appropriate designs for seeking answers to the questions. We will next take a look at some of the basic measurement issues involved in planning and implementing reading research studies.

Careful designing of the study eliminates, or at least minimizes, most of the basic measurement issues, especially those associated with the analysis of data. All too frequently, however, reading researchers proceed with data collecting and then attempt to search out appropriate ways of quantifying and analyzing the results of their efforts. Sets of test scores or other measurements collected in a hit or miss fashion, or used because they are readily available, do not lend themselves to meaningful analyses and interpretation.

However, no matter how carefully a study is designed, quite unexpected problems may arise. As good researchers, we are challenged to anticipate these problems and to be prepared to meet them. What are some of the major sources that may contribute to research error? In discussing the reduction of error variance, McNemar (1962, p. 382) classifies errors under three headings: "measuring or observational errors, errors in inferring population parameters in field or survey studies, and errors in experimental testing of hypotheses." The first of these errors concerns the reliability of the instrument used for data collection; the second involves selecting samples that are unbiased and representative of the defined population; and the third deals with problems discussed by Wardrop in the Spring 1971 issue of the *Reading Research Quarterly*. Among the many problems which continue to vex reading researchers, Wardrop (p. 332) has identified three major ones that frequently appear in reading research reports. These are "design/analysis mismatch, inadequate specification of treatment, and control groups that do not 'control'."

Other problems related to these basic categories are practical as well as statistical in nature. Frequently, the statistical problems are more readily resolved than the practical ones. Farr and Tuinman include some of the practical issues in their article "The Dependent Variable: Measurement Issues in Reading Research," which appeared in the Spring 1972 issue of the *Reading Research Quarterly*. These authors (p. 415) grouped measurement problems into four major categories: "the selection and validation of appropriate measures, the reliability of assessments, the appropriate scores to use, and the description of tests and testing conditions." This list can be extended to include problems involved in identifying the population and selecting the sample, in implementing the study, in assessing changes in reading behavior, and in designing studies utilizing complex statistical techniques such as factor analysis and matrix sampling.

In their very thorough treatise "Experimental and Quasi-Experimental Designs for Research on Teaching," Campbell and Stanley (1963) identify twelve factors which may jeopardize the validity of various experimental designs. They distinguish between *internal validity* and *external validity*. In doing a controlled study, we may want to know if the experimental treatments result in a difference in performance of the subjects within the experimental setting. We would be concerned with *internal validity* and the factors which may operate to lessen the internal validity of the experiment. In planning the study and in drawing conclusions, we would want to know to what populations, what other settings, and which treatment variable and measurement variables the observed effects can be generalized. Here we are interested in generalizability, or in Campbell and Stanley's terms, *external validity*. Those authors go on to identify eight different classes of extraneous variables that are relevant to internal validity and four relevant to external validity. These, in turn, are illustrated through presentation of sixteen experimental designs.

From this variety of factors, I have selected for consideration several which are relevant to many kinds of reading research, and I have grouped them as follows:
1. Some sampling problems
2. Selecting the data-gathering instrument
3. Problems in the field
4. Selecting the appropriate score mode
5. Measuring change

Some sampling problems

The sample is an integral component of the research design and has direct bearing both on the choice of statistical techniques to be applied in treating the data and on the generalizations that can be drawn from the results. Guidelines for sampling are provided in current statistics textbooks and journal articles. According to McNemar (1962, p. 382), "The aim is to secure a sample which is unbiased, that is, representative of a defined population, with chance sampling errors as small as possible." The problems of minimizing sampling errors are related to the type of study being planned. The errors which may arise in large scale sampling as in survey and norming studies may be quite different from the sampling errors that may arise when groups are selected for experimental purposes.

One of the first steps in sampling is to define the population to be sampled. A researcher investigating some aspect of early school reading might define the population as children entering the first grade during the fall of the school year. Subpopulations within this larger one could be identified as those children entering public schools and those entering private schools, or as those having had earlier school experiences and those with no school experiences. In selecting a sample that is to be representative of the population and in identifying control groups that will operate effectively, consideration must be given to very practical factors such as the accessibility of subjects, the kinds of experimental conditions to be imposed, and the amount of time, effort, and money required to collect the desired information. If repeated measurements are to be obtained, mobility of the population from which the sample is to be drawn is an important factor. Attrition is particularly crucial when small samples are involved.

Failure to recognize the need for careful identification of the sample before starting to collect data is demonstrated in letters like the following: "Dear Sir: I am undertaking a research study in reading. A nearby school administered one of your reading tests in the fall. Could you please tell me if there is a second form available, so I can retest these pupils in the spring?" In this situation, economy of using an available sample seems to be of prime consideration. Upon careful investigation, it may turn out that this intact group is most inappropriate for the purposes of the study.

The size of the sample is also an important consideration and is directly related to the type of research that is being conducted. To quote McNemar (1962, p. 84), "One of the aims of scientific method is to attain as great precision in results as is practical." In experimental settings, as well as in survey and norming studies, greater precision is usually obtained by increasing the size of the sample. However, it is *how well* the sample represents the population rather than size, per se, that leads to meaningful generalizations. Through careful planning, it may be possible to attain an acceptable degree of precision without unduly increasing the size of the sample.

The sampling unit is related to the size of the sample and to the statistical technique to be applied in analyzing the data. Is the sampling unit to be individuals drawn randomly from a given population, or intact groups such as classrooms? In applying analysis of variance, for example, data collected from classes selected randomly should not be treated as though they were derived from a random sample of individuals because classes not individuals are the sampling units.

In defining the sample, all variables which may influence the results of an experiment should be isolated and controlled. Consideration should be given to possible effects of age, sex, grade placement, mental ability, type of school system, previous learning experiences, and ethnic or regional differences and related socioeconomic factors. For example, previous learning experiences may have important bearing on the effects of treatments to be applied in a learning experiment at the second grade level. In population of grade two pupils, all pupils may not have had similar reading experiences during the first grade. The group might be quite heterogeneous in the sense that some had learned to read in a program using the linguistic approach, others in a phonics program, and the rest in a basal reader program stressing the whole word approach.

The final research report should fully describe the samples and the population from which they were drawn. The characteristics of the sample have direct bearing on the kinds of generalizations that can be drawn from the results and are necessary information if the study is to be replicated.

Selecting the data gathering instrument

If a reading study is to provide meaningful information, the instruments to be used in collecting the information must be carefully selected. The three basic characteristics to consider in choosing an instrument are *validity, reliability,* and *usability.* The first two of these are treated in most basic measurement texts and in the Farr and Tuinman article referred to earlier. The third characteristic, usability, encompasses problems encountered in administering the test. Such problems must be taken into consideration at the time the data-collecting device is being planned. If implementation of the study is to involve teachers or others in the collection of data, then the directions, timing, and other administrative procedures must be controlled so that errors resulting from the test administration itself are kept to a minimum.

There are several sources for locating tests that have the desired characteristics. Ideally, an instrument designed specifically to fit the aims of the study will yield the most valid information. However, development of an instrument involves extensive pilot work and field testing to ensure that it will function as desired. It generally takes from three to five years to bring a major reading test battery from the initial planning stage to the point where all the components are available for use. Usually, the time needed to develop a data-collecting instrument for a reading research study is considerably less than this. However, anyone contemplating the development of a series of reading tests for a factor analytic study may find that solving the problems of item refinement, subtest reliabilities and subtest intercorrelations are the major tasks in the project. An interesting discussion of some of the issues involved in factor analytic studies of reading, can be found in an article by Thorndike entitled "Reading as

Reasoning" which appeared in the 1974 issue of the *Reading Research Quarterly*.

A search of the literature may reveal the existence of reading instruments that have been refined and field tested in other research studies. Another convenient source is the commercially published test. In examining ready-made instruments, the first consideration is that of validity. Will the instrument provide relevant information about the reading skill, instructional technique, or other variable that is being investigated?

The title of a test or a brief description will not convey all the necessary information. A test of listening comprehension, for example, may have a response mode that is heavily loaded with reading, or the item type may be tapping skills other than those you plan to study. The test manual usually describes the rationale of the test and provides information on the validity and reliability of the test for its recommended uses. In addition to studying the rationale and the procedures used in developing the test, the potential user should examine carefully the item types to see if they elicit the kinds of behavior the test purports to measure. By actually taking the test in accord with prescribed directions, the reviewer may discover that the methods used in presenting the stimuli do not tap the desired behavior or that the test is inappropriate for the maturity level of the children in the sample. In his text, *The Specification and Measurement of Learning Outcomes,* Payne (1968, p. 52) presents a list of critical questions to be used in reviewing test items. His book, as well as others in the measurement area, provides practical information on designing a test.

Articles which report on the use of the instrument in other studies may provide information about the reliability of the test with selected samples and may suggest ways in which the instrument can be improved if it is to be used in subsequent studies. Buros' *Mental Measurements Yearbooks* are valuable sources of information about published tests. In the Yearbooks, brief descriptions of a test usually accompany reviews written by measurement and content specialists. These reviews, as well as those which have appeared in professional journals and reading texts, will help you to decide on the appropriateness of the test for your study. Also, the test author or publisher may have collected validity and reliability information subsequent to the publication of a test. When available, reports from these sources should give you a better understanding of the test.

Often, one or more subtests or a set of items from a research or published test may provide the kinds of information that you are seeking. A test may be lengthened to increase its reliability, or the directions altered to fit the conditions of your experiment. If the test materials are copyrighted, permission must be obtained before they can be adapted. To avoid delays and possible misunderstandings, the request to adapt a test should be presented to the author or publisher during the planning of the project and before final decisions are made. All too often, an urgent request comes in for permission to adapt copyrighted material for use almost immediately.

Reliability of the measurements is the concern of all researchers. McNemar (1962, p. 382) states that "errors of measurement can be reduced by developing more reliable tests or (when feasible) by averaging repeated measurements." Since the reliability of a test for a given situation is related to the variability of the scores obtained, a test may not be equally reliable in all situations. In developing or adapting an instrument, the researcher faces the problem of estimating the reliability of the instrument before administering it in the experimental situation. If the samples reported in estimating the reliability of a published test differ significantly from those in your study, then the appropriateness of the reported reliabilities may be questionable. In either case, reliability values should be computed and included in the final research report.

Problems in the field

Once the reading experiment is designed, the sample identified, and the appropriate data gathering instrument is at hand, all that remains is for the research to be implemented. It is in this phase that many of the more practical measurement-related problems arise, especially if the study is to be conducted in classrooms or other school situations.

Careful arrangements must be made to insure that the subjects selected for the sample will be available throughout the entire experimental period; that appropriate facilities are available; and that teachers, parents, and, in as far as possible, the children themselves understand the purpose of the study and the extent of their involvement.

There may be times within the school year or even within the school day that are inappropriate for the experiment you are planning. For example, the period between Thanksgiving and Christmas is usually a busy time for most teachers.

Does your project call for special training, a series of conferences, or other commitments from members of the school staff? If so, the nature and extent of these involvements should be made clear and agreements reached before the project is started.

Even though thorough planning has taken place, administrative procedures have been routinized, and time schedules have been carefully adhered to, unanticipated events will arise which may have an effect on the sample as originally defined, on the procedures for implementing the study, or on the interpretations and generalizations which may ensue from the results. Occurrences of this kind should be recorded and attention given to the effect they may possibly have.

Selecting the appropriate score mode

The appropriate score to be used in quantifying and analyzing the information gathered in a research study depends on a variety of factors. The discussion here is limited to the kinds of scores usually associated with standardized tests. Decisions as to the score mode to be used should be reached before the instrument is administered and the scores are generated.

If descriptive or control data are to be transcribed from school records or other sources, the type of score that is available and the completeness of the records should be investigated before the final decision is made to use these data. It may happen that only derived scores are available when you intended to use raw scores. A plaintive letter like this one may reveal a problem which should have been anticipated: "Dear Sir: In carrying out my reading research study, I planned to use IQ as one of the control variables. To cut down on testing time and costs, I am using IQs which had been entered on the pupil records during the past two years. Unfortunately, I now find that about three-fourths of the pupils took one intelligence test, the rest an intelligence test published by another company. Do you have conversion tables that I can use to equate these two sets of IQs?" Usually, there is little that can be done to help in situations like this.

In general, raw scores are more appropriate statistically than derived scores. However, if alternate forms or sequential levels of a test are administered, then scaled or standard scores, when available, would be appropriate. Raw scores and standard scores, however, may be difficult to interpret in a curricular or instructional sense. Farr and Tuinman (1972, p. 420) suggest that for practical purposes, the results be analyzed first in terms of raw score differences and then translated into grade equivalents, percentile ranks, or other derived score differences. For example, a difference in grade equivalents of 8 months, or a stanine difference of 2 may be more readily understood and applied than a raw score difference of 12 points. However, in interpreting results in terms of derived scores, the researcher should be aware of underlying assumptions and any limitations of the derived score modes.

Measuring change

Reading researchers are usually more concerned with investigations in an experimental setting than with large-scale or normative studies. Their designs sometimes call for the identification of control and experimental groups and may involve the assessment of changes in behavior under specified conditions. With recent emphasis on accountability in education, there have been increasing attempts within schools and by external evaluators to administer pretests and posttests and to assess and account for the amount of change that has taken place during a prescribed period of instruction.

In a Test Service Notebook entitled *Accountability in Education and Associated Measurement Problems,* Wrightstone, Hogan, and Abbott discuss measurement problems associated with accountability in education. These authors first define accountability and then lead into a discussion of two kinds of problems—those involved in determining the status of a pupil or group of pupils at one time during the year and those related to changes in performance over an instructional period. Academic growth is defined operationally as "the numerical difference of two sets of scores" (p. 5). Since this article identifies special problems associated with changes in academic performance and offers possible approaches to their solution, the points discussed are pertinent to anyone contemplating a gains study.

What are some of the issues that should concern a researcher interested in assessing changes in reading behavior? In his text, *Educational Measurements and Their Interpretations,* Davis (1964) provides some basic guidelines when change is to be measured by subtracting pretest scores from posttest scores. He states, "This method of measuring change is appropriate if the test forms are highly reliable, if the pupil or pupils were not selected for training on the basis of initial score, and if the estimate of change for the pupil or groups of pupils is not to be compared with changes in the scores of pupils or groups of pupils whose initial scores were markedly different." He continues, "The best measure of change in an individual is an estimate of the *true* change" (p. 251).

Among the problems associated with measurement change is that of determining the amount of time to intervene between testings. There must be sufficient time for learning to take place if the differences are to represent real gains. If the time interval is relatively short, or if there are other uncontrollable factors which may affect the test scores at the end of the learning experiment, then alternate forms of the test should be administered at the beginning and the end of the experiment. If this is the plan, it must be determined in advance that alternate forms are available and that they are comparable in design and content and yield equivalent scores. This issue is of real concern to researchers who develop their own instruments or adapt standardized tests in such a way that pre-established interform relationships no longer hold.

During the preschool and primary years, reading skills may be developing so rapidly that the level of the test administered at the beginning of the experiment may not be appropriate as the final test. If a relatively easy test is given at the beginning of the assessment, there may not be sufficient ceiling when it is used as a posttest. In developing or selecting a multilevel instrument as a solution to this issue, the problem of developing scores equivalent from level to level has to be recognized and resolved.

Implicit in the Davis guidelines and the concerns expressed by Wrightstone and his coauthors are the issues of regression toward the mean and reliability of difference scores. When the same test scores are used to place pupils in the research program and again as pretest scores to be compared later with posttest scores, the problem of regression occurs. The differences in scores reflect not only the real gains but also the effects of any regression that may have taken place.

Fortunately, problems of regression can be avoided through careful planning. One approach is to identify pupils for the research program by some means other than the test used in gathering the data. A different test or a different set of criteria can be used to select the students. Also, when careful attention is given to matching design and analysis techniques, the problems of measuring change are reduced. The effects of regression can then be controlled through the use of appropriate statistical techniques.

Problems of reliability of gain scores have been vexing reading researchers for years. In a guest editorial for the Spring 1971 issue of the *Reading Research Quarterly,* Stake and Wardrop vividly illustrate that the unreliability of gain scores for individuals can give the appearance of learning when no learning has taken place. Many statistical texts cover this topic in detail. Both Davis and Wrightstone present examples which help to clarify the concepts of regression and reliability of difference scores.

There is no simple approach which will resolve all the measurement problems which may arise. This discussion has recognized the importance of formulating the problem and asking appropriate questions and the importance of a design that will provide reliable and valid information about the problem. In addition, measurement issues typifying those that many reading researchers will face have been identified. However, there are others which may be more significant to a specific research project. Good researchers must anticipate practical as well as statistical problems that may arise and be prepared to cope with them.

REFERENCES

BUROS, O. K. (Ed.). *The seventh mental measurements yearbook.* Highland Park, New Jersey: Gryphon Press, 1972.

CAMPBELL, DONALD T., & STANLEY, JULIAN C. Experimental and quasi-experimental designs for research on teaching. In N. L. Gage (Ed.) *Handbook of Research on Teaching.* Chicago: Rand McNally, 1963. Pp. 171-246.

CRONBACH, LEE J.; GLESER, GOLDINE C.; NANDA, HARINDER; & RAJARATNAM, NAGESEVARI. *The dependability of behavior measurements: theory of generalizability for scores and profiles.* New York: John Wiley and Sons, 1972.

DAVIS, FREDERICK B. *Educational measurements and their interpretation.* Belmont, California: Wadsworth, 1964.

FARR, ROGER, & TUINMAN, J. JAAP. The dependent variable: measurement issues in reading research. *Reading Research Quarterly,* Spring 1972, *7*, 413-423.

Mc NEMAR, QUINN. *Psychological statistics,* New York: John Wiley and Sons, 1962.

PAYNE, DAVID A. *The specification and measurement of learning outcomes.* Waltham, Massachusetts: Blaisdell, 1968.

STAKE, ROBERT E., & WARDROP, JAMES L. Performance contracts and test errors. *Reading Research Quarterly,* Spring 1971, *6*, 323-325.

THORNDIKE, ROBERT L. Reading as reasoning. *Reading Research Quarterly,* 1974, *9*, 137-147.

WARDROP, JAMES L. Some particularly vexing problems in experimentation on reading. *Reading Research Quarterly,* Spring 1971, *6*, 329-337.

WARDROP, JAMES L., & ESSEX, DIANE L. Vexing problems revisited: pitfalls for the unwary researcher (A reaction to Kennedy and Weener). *Reading Research Quarterly,* Summer 1973, *8*, 542-557.

WRIGHTSTONE, J. WAYNE; HOGAN, THOMAS P.; & ABBOTT, MURIEL M. Accountability in education and associated measurement problems. *Test Service Notebook 33.* New York: Harcourt Brace Jovanovich.

Conducting longitudinal research in reading

KATHRYN A. BLAKE
JERRY C. ALLEN
University of Georgia

Description of longitudinal research

Longitudinal research is one method for studying how and why pupil behavior changes over a relatively long time period. In longitudinal research, we have two purposes. The first purpose is to *describe* how pupil behavior changes as time passes or as pupils participate in particular treatments as time passes. That is, we analyze and portray the nature of the curve, showing rate of behavioral change as a function of time or time and treatments in combination. The second purpose is to *ascribe* those behavioral changes to particular independent events which occurred during the time span studied. That is, we interpret the behavior we described.

Longitudinal studies are often called growth studies or developmental studies. Growth studies are very important in gaining information to increase the effectiveness of education. As van Dalen (1973, p. 241) pointed out:

> To teach effectively, one must have knowledge of the nature and rate of changes that take place in human organisms. One must know what interrelated factors affect growth at various stages of development; when various aspects of growth are first observable, spurt forward, remain rather stationary, reach optimal development, and decline; and how the duration, intensity, and timing of an experience in the developmental period affect growth.

Longitudinal research is only one method for studying how behavior changes over a longer period of time. Other methods are the cross-sectional method, the semilongitudinal method, and the retrospective method. Let's look at longitudinal research in relation to these other three methods.

The *longitudinal method* involves making a number of repeated observations on the *same* subjects as they progress through a number of time periods. For example, to study pupil growth in interpreting figurative language, pupil response to idioms, metaphors, similes, and other devices could be sampled when the pupils are at Grade 1, Grade 2, Grade 3, and so on. Then, this group's average scores for each successive year could be joined to make a growth curve.

The *cross-sectional method* involves making one observation on *different* subjects at a number of levels. For example, to study pupil growth in reading comprehension skills, measurements could be made at one given time for a group of pupils at Grade 1, another group at Grade 2, another at Grade 3, and so on. Then, the several groups' average scores could be joined to make a growth curve.

The *semi-longitudinal method* is a combination of the longitudinal method and the cross-sectional method. It involves measuring the *same* subjects at a given level at least twice over a period of time (and sometimes more) and measuring *different* subjects at different levels. For example, to study pupil growth in sight vocabulary, measurement could be made in the fall and the spring of a given year for a group of first graders, for a group of second graders, a group of third graders, and so on. Then, each group's curve for a year could be joined to other groups' curves to make a long-term growth curve.

The *retrospective approach* involves using reports of past behavior rather than observations of present and future behavior. People, such as parents, who have known the pupils describe how their behavior was at various times. For example, to show pupils' early progress in reading, the parents could recount the ages when their children first became attentive to words; when they first started to read road signs, labels, and similar materials; their initial responses to instruction in school; and so on.

All of these approaches are useful in dealing with questions about longer-term behavior changes. Each has its values and its limitations. The topic for this paper is longitudinal research and that is what we will consider from here on. We will look at illustrations, concepts, interpretations, and research questions and designs.

Illustrations of longitudinal research

Among the classic longitudinal studies are Bayley's research on intellectual growth from infancy through old age and the Terman group's research on highly intelligent children's growth in various areas from childhood through old age. Instances of longitudinal research in reading include work by Bond and Dykstra (1967), Bruininks and Lucker (1970), Mazurkiewicz (1971), and Satz (1974). More broadly, the historical perspective is shown in Stone and Onque's survey (1959) of time-series research for the past one hundred years. A current example in education is the work of the American Institutes for Research (A.I.R.) with Project Talent subjects who are now in their 30s. In 1960, the A.I.R. group started with about 400,000 randomly selected pupils. The plan is to observe students at various periods after their high school graduation to see how much the education and counselling they received helped them in later life. The National Institute of Education recently granted funds for another stage in the study.

To get a clearer picture, let's look in more detail at Bayley's longitudinal work on the growth of intellectual abilities from infancy through the life span. The research has yielded some information which has important implications for reading instruction. For example, her information about adult intelligence has implications for reading improvement in post-high school students and other adults. In the past, one notion has been that intelligence is a unitary, or general, ability in which growth levels off in late adolescence. If this were so, then we could hypothesize that growth in reading skills related to intelligence would also level off in late adolescence. However, Bayley (1966, 1968, 1970) has shown that intellectual growth continues into adulthood, that there are different intellectual abilities which show different patterns of growth, and that males and females show different rates and levels of intellectual growth. The growth curves in Figure 1 show these patterns of development in intellectual abilities during the age period between CA 16 and CA 36.

Bayley (1970) made these comments about her data.

> From these studies again we have evidence for multiple mental abilities, which develop in different ways. Some show more continuous growth than others. Some are more consistent over time than others. It appears that one general class of abilities, which may be referred to as verbal facility and knowledge, is not only more stable within individuals throughout growth but also continues to increase in adults to 30 years of age or older. Other abilities appear to be more bound to stage of development, to be less stable over time, and to reach their peak in the twenties. Such fluid abilities include reasoning processes, arithmetic and verbal reasoning, perhaps attention span or short-term memory and speed [p. 1185].

To the extent that abilities sampled by the Wechsler Scales are related to reading skills, Bayley's information indicates that we can hypothesize: that older adolescents and younger adults could continue to develop in

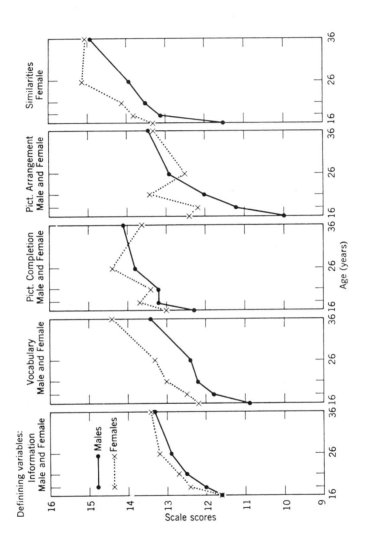

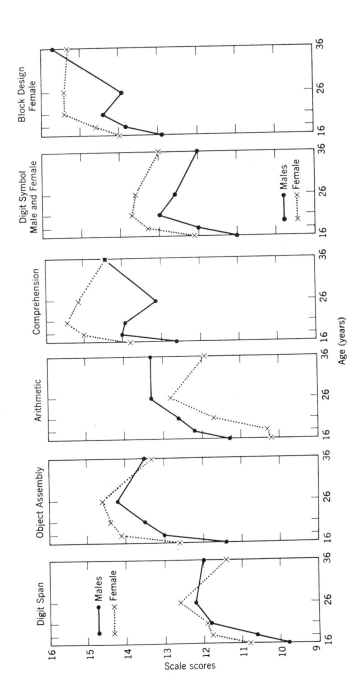

Figure 1. Growth Curves for Various Mental Abilities (Wechsler Intelligence Scales)

Source: Nancy Bayley, "Development of Mental Abilities. In Paul H. Mussen (Ed.), *Carmichael's Manual of Child Psychology*, Vol. 1. New York: Wiley, 1970. Pp. 1184-1185.

reading—that is, to show higher levels in acquiring comprehension, interpretation, evaluation, and processing skills in reading and in learning to apply those skills in dealing with problems—and that males and females would show different patterns of learning such skills.

Concepts pertaining to longitudinal research

Questions in longitudinal research

Longitudinal research can be used in answering several types of questions. In this paper, we will consider design, analysis, and interpretation for two types: questions about how a particular characteristic changes over a period of time as students grow older or participate in certain common experiences with time, like schooling; questions about how a characteristic changes as students participate over a period of time in particular treatments, that is, any instructional procedure or other experience designed to cause changes in behavior. These types of questions can be asked with a cross-section of students. Or they can be asked about particular groups of students who are selected to be different on a particular subject characteristic and homogeneous on other relevant characteristics, for example: males and females; pupils from English speaking backgrounds and pupils from non-English speaking backgrounds.

> *Changes with time*
> Does pupil behavior change over a period of time?
> Do different groups of pupils show different patterns of behavior change over a period of time?
> *Changes with time and treatments*
> Does a given treatment affect pupil behavior over a period of time?
> Do different groups of pupils respond differently to a given treatment over a period of time?

These questions, of course, are stated in general form. In particular research projects, they would be more specific to reflect the situation.

Designing longitudinal research

There is a research design for each longitudinal research question. A research design is a plan for collecting data needed to answer a question. It shows the arrangement of the variables.

The *independent variable* is the variable whose influence on a dependent variable is being studied. In longitudinal research, time is the main independent variable. As Holtzman (1963) commented:

Any approach to the study of change must involve two or more measurements of the same variable at different times in order to provide a basis for inferring that change has or has not taken place. In all such designs, time is the master variable against which everything else is ordered [p. 199].

Other independent variables are subject variables and treatment variables. Subject variables are characteristics of the pupils. Subject variables of interest in reading research include such characteristics as visual acuity, auditory acuity, intellectual ability, mental maturity, language facility, cognitive style, motivational style, and so on through a wide range of variables. Treatment variables are methods, materials, and other procedures designed to influence the dependent variable. Treatment variables in reading research include such procedures as emphasis on decoding skills, alternation of type size and style, use of advance organizers, manipulation of redundancy, timing of prereading experiences, variation of syntactic structures, arrangement of generalizations and specific instances, and so on through myriad possibilities.

The *dependent variable* is the variable which may be influenced by the independent variable. In reading research, these could be any aspect of reading behavior or any aspect of behavior related to reading, for example, skill in visual discrimination, knowledge of phonics rules, understanding of the meaning of unbound morphemes, grasp of concepts, memory for sentences in various transformations, skill in finding ideas, facility in detecting relations, familiarity with literary genre, and so on through a very large number of variables.

Control variables are the variables which are not under study but which could enter in to affect the dependent variable and lead to erroneous conclusions about the influence of the independent variable. These, of course, vary with the independent and dependent variables being studied.

As with other research approaches, the chief criterion for an adequate design in longitudinal research is: The procedures for dealing with all of the variables should be such that the data obtained will yield unequivocal, valid answers to the research question about the independent and dependent variables being studied. In later sections, we will consider threats to validity which can operate in several designs. If we plan adequate ways to circumvent these threats to validity and if we can demonstrate that we did circumvent them, then we can make valid generalizations following from the research question.

Analysis of longitudinal data

Once we obtain our data, we are ready to analyze them. As noted, the first purpose of longitudinal research is to *describe* change which takes place in the dependent variable as time passes or as pupils are exposed to particular treatments as time passes. We seek to make four kinds of inferences when we describe change with time in longitudinal research. Here are the inferences accompanied by the evidence stated in statistical and in non-statistical terms. For illustration, the material is keyed to Figure 1 showing some of Bayley's longitudinal research results.

To make inferences about whether a change occurs. Does the slope of the curve differ from zero: Is there a trend? Does the dependent variable change? Note that Bayley's curves are not flat. All have slopes which depart from zero. We can infer that intellectual abilities do change between CA's 16 and 36.

If a change occurs, to make inferences about the nature of the change. Is there a linear trend: Is there an equal change in the dependent variable for each change in time? Is there a quadratic trend: Is there an unequal change in the dependent variable for each change in time? Is the rate of change positively accelerated, that is, increasing with time? Is the rate of change negatively accelerated, that is, decreasing with time? Is the trend cubic, is it quartic, etc.: Is there more than one inflection point where rate of change varies as it happens when pupils grow, reach plateaus, and start growing again? Bayley's curves suggest that females generally show a linear trend in vocabulary growth between CA's 16 and 36. We can infer that they show equal increments in vocabulary between testing periods. The other trends are non-linear. During the 20-year period, the groups show various patterns on increments, plateaus, and decrements on the different abilities.

To make inferences about whether subject groups or treatment groups show similar trends. Do the slopes of the curves differ in displacement: Do the groups differ? Are the slopes parallel: Do the groups show the same rates and patterns of change? Bayley's curves suggest that males and females show similar patterns of growth on the characteristic sampled by the Information Scale and different patterns in the other abilities. Note especially the two groups' relative positions and patterns on Arithmetic *vis a vis* the other scales, especially Vocabulary, Similarities, and Comprehension.

To make inferences or projections about how trends will continue. Given a trend, what values can we expect through given future time periods? In no case did Bayley's groups reach the top of the scales. Consider what we might expect from the next 10- or 20-year periods in abilities like vocabulary in contrast to abilities like immediate memory (Digit Span).

We base these inferences about concrete behavior on data at two levels of abstraction. At the first level are scores on instruments used to sample the dependent variable and, in some situations, the independent and control variables. We obtain these data by measurement procedures

Conducting longitudinal research

designated psychometric procedures. At the second level of abstraction are statistical indices we obtain by analyzing the scores with particular statistical procedures in four categories: procedures for describing individuals, correlational procedures including regression analysis, analysis of variance procedures including co-variance analysis, and multivariate procedures.

Each psychometric and statistical procedure has its requirements, values, and limitations. Problems in psychometric procedures and statistical procedures compound with problems in design procedures to create some major difficulties in getting unequivocal enough data to accurately describe the change which takes place in reality. In short, different combinations of procedures used to describe the same phenomenon can lead to different results. Therefore, procedures need to be weighed and chosen carefully to get the soundest results possible with the fewest restrictions. Bereiter's comments (1963) illustrate some difficulties:

> The writer [Bereiter] had the privilege of working with the Vassar studies of personality and attitude changes during the college years. Most of the quantitative data were obtained from two administrations of the same test battery, once in the freshman year and once in the senior year. Some pronounced general changes were observed, and a natural question to ask was whether these changes occurred at an even rate throughout the four years or whether they were mostly accomplished during the first years. Since yearly retesting of the same persons could probably have a serious contaminating effect, samples of one class were retested at various times—some at the end of their freshman year, some at the end of their sophomore year, and so on. As often happens, however, the subjects, though invited at random, did not accept randomly and it turned out that samples retested in different years differed significantly in freshman scores. What to make of this? We could ignore the discrepancies between initial scores and merely plot the retest means for the various groups as a function of time of retesting and try to fit a continuous curve of change to it. Or we could, by any number of devices, attempt to adjust the retest scores to compensate for differences in initial scores. Depending on the decision, we could get the curves to look almost any way we like— linear, negatively accelerated, S-shaped, or what have you.
>
> In another part of the Vassar studies we were concerned with differences among curricular groups. Two questions were of interest: a) Do different fields attract different kinds of students? and b) Do students change differently during college depending on their major field of study? The answer to the first question was unequivocally "yes" and this made it difficult to answer the second question. Several related measures of "attitude growth" were available. When raw change was used, it turned out that the *lower* groups were initially, the more they gained during college. When the initial score on any one

measure was partialed out, it was found that the *higher* groups were on related measures, the more they gained. This complete reversal of findings when the switch is made from raw to corrected change scores seems to be typical, and it is difficult not to be suspicious of it, to suspect that it represents a switch from one kind of error to another [p. 4].

The point here is that to perform or evaluate longitudinal research, you need to be familiar with such problems. You can gain such knowledge in psychometrics or statistics courses and in books like Annastasi (1968), Cronbach (1970), Edwards (1968), and Weiner (1971).

Interpretation of longitudinal data

As noted, the second purpose of longitudinal research is to *ascribe* the changes we observe in the dependent variable to the independent variables, that is, to particular events which occur during the time span studied. Such interpretation can be rather tricky business. As Campbell (1963) pointed out:

We have examined the methodology of asking: "Did a change take place here?" "What attributes changed?" "What things tend to change together?" "What is the general, normal, change or growth pattern for this animal, this person, this group, this institution?" "How do change patterns vary as concomitants of social settings?" The problems encountered at this level are so formidable that it may seem gratuitous to ask a still more ambitious one. So frequently do data processing procedures mislead us in answering the question "Did a change occur?" that we should perhaps hesitate before jumping to ask "What caused the change?"

Yet, in the literature, the methodology which we are seeking to improve, this reticence is usually lacking. Few describe change without attempting to explain it. Most undertake the research assuming in advance that they know the causal agent, asking only the question of the degree of efficacy: be it of genetic patterns, of maturation, Vassar College, military experience, psychotherapy, remedial reading, or what not [p. 212].

Interpreting longitudinal data is the same as interpreting data obtained with other research methods. We can accept hypotheses about the causal influence of our independent variables only when plausible rival hypotheses have been ruled out. That is, once we *describe* the relationships which exist and then seek to *ascribe* them to our independent variables, we go through three steps.

- Formulate hypotheses about all of the variables in the situation which could cause changes in the dependent variable. These hypotheses include hypotheses about the independent variables.

And these hypotheses include rival hypotheses about other, extraneous variables which could be influencing the dependent variable and thus be a threat to the validity of the study, that is, to the extent to which the data will yield unequivocal answers to the research question about the independent variables and dependent variable being studied.

- Present evidence to discount the rival hypotheses. Given sufficient evidence, reject these rival hypotheses.
- Accept the hypotheses about the independent variables.

To be able to carry out these three steps, we need to plan ahead when we are setting up a longitudinal study. We need to anticipate what variables in addition to the independent variables could enter in to influence the dependent variable and thus become rival hypotheses or threats to the validity of the study. Then, we need to use appropriate procedures to deal with these potentially problem variables. Several authors (Campbell and Stanley, 1963, pp. 171-241; Bracht and Glass, 1968, pp. 437-474; van Dalen, 1974, pp. 259-361) have described variables to consider and procedures for dealing with rival hypotheses or threats to validity. The material below describes some variables or threats to *internal* validity which need to be planned for in the longitudinal research designs involving groups and treatments described below. (To keep down the complexity and length of this chapter, threats to *external* validity are not discussed herein. However, they merit consideration.)

History.   Sometimes, specific events take place between the times measurements are made, and these events operate in addition to the independent variable to influence the dependent variables. For example, suppose we were studying the effect of the Frostig program for training visual perception on the development of young children's visual discrimination performance. If the children were concurrently watching *Sesame Street,* we would not know whether to ascribe changes to the Frostig program, *Sesame Street,* or both. Dealing with history as a threat to internal validity involves two procedures:

- When treatments are being studied, use a control group who does not get the treatment but who would experience the specific events. Differences between the treatment and control groups could then be attributed to the treatment, other things being equal.
- In studies involving treatments and in those not involving treatments, specify variables which could enter in to confound the results; explicitly survey whether the subjects experienced those variables; and, if so, limit generalizations appropriately.

Psychological changes.   Over time, subjects may change in ways which have nothing to do with the independent variable. That is, they may lose interest in the study, they may acquire a particular enthusiasm for the study, and so on. For example, suppose we used an audiovisual program for teaching vocabulary that had a large novelty appeal for younger pupils but not for older ones. Changes in the dependent variable might decline over the time period because of differential interest, not because of decreasing effectiveness of the program. Here are three procedures appropriate to deal with psychological changes as a threat to internal validity:

- In treatment studies, use a control group which does not take part in the treatment but does partake in equally interesting parallel activities.
- In both treatment and in nontreatment studies, identify attitudes and interests which might influence the dependent variable; survey them several times during the study; and, if they operate, restrict generalizations appropriately.
- In all studies, choose treatment methods which would not be subject to changes in interest, etc. If possible, spend a warm-up period giving subjects experience with the situation so that the novelty would dissipate before the study starts.

Responses to tests. The term *test* may be used broadly to refer to any procedure for sampling the dependent variable, for example, paper and pencil instruments, ratings, interviews, mechanical devices, etc. Sometimes, testing influences subjects in a way that affects their later responses to the tests: they may learn what is expected, they may be traumatized, they may have their interest aroused, and so on. For example, suppose a reading test given first to beginning first graders involved pupils' making, for them, a fairly complex response like completion or filling in the blanks. The pupils could score spuriously low on the first test and then higher subsequently when they learn how to respond. Such improvement could not be ascribed correctly to the independent variable. Procedures for dealing with testing as a threat to validity include:

- Use the same test throughout the study if possible.
- Train pupils in the mechanics of responding to the tests before the tests are administered in the research situation.
- Use control subjects who receive the tests but not the treatment.

Changes in tests. Over time, tests may undergo various changes like changes in calibration, observers, alternate forms, and revisions. Such changes may affect the obtained measures of the dependent variable. For example, children might be given one form of a reading test when they are at the primary reading levels and another form when they are at the intermediate reading levels. If the two forms differed in relative difficulty, differences in the dependent variable could not be ascribed entirely to the independent variable. Several procedures for dealing with changes in tests as a threat are:

- Calibrate mechanical devices to a norm before each testing period.
- Use standard procedures for raters and observers and have training sessions at the outset of each testing period. Assign subjects randomly to raters and observers or vice versa. Be sure all subjects are exposed to different researchers over time or conversely that no researcher deals exclusively with a particular group of subjects.
- Use only alternate test forms which are demonstrated to be equated.
- Use tests where subsequent forms are carefully calibrated to shade into one another and not vary in relative difficulty.
- Use control subjects who receive the tests but not the treatments.

Statistical regression. When groups have been selected on the basis of scores which are above the mean or average, the scores they obtain when they are retested will move lower toward the mean. Groups chosen for the scores below the mean will show the reverse pattern. These changes are manifestations of statistical regression. They might seem to be the effect of the independent variable; however, they occur because of psychometric and statistical phenomena. For example, suppose a group of poor readers were chosen for a remedial treatment, with poor readers being defined as pupils two grade-levels below the average in reading achievement for their age group. On retesting, their mean scores could move toward the average regardless of the influence of the independent variable—the remedial reading program. Dealing with statistical regression as a threat includes procedures like the following:

- In treatment studies, use a control group.
- In studies not involving treatments, attribute the changes toward the population mean to the possible influence of statistical regression in addition to the influence of the independent variable.

Differential selection of groups. Groups may be used in two ways: in studies of independent subject variables and in studies of treatments. Groups used in these ways must show certain similarities and differences on variables related to the dependent variable:

- When groups are used to study the effect of an independent subject variable on a dependent variable, these groups should differ on the independent variable and be equivalent on all control variables, that is, on all other subject characteristics related to the dependent variable and all experiences which could influence the dependent variable. Otherwise, given differences on these other variables, these differences might enter in to influence the dependent variable and confuse the results. For example, suppose we were comparing the reading growth of pupils high in need achievement with the reading growth of pupils low in need achievement. Differences in reading growth could not be attributed to differences in need achievement level if the pupils also differed on related variables like initial status in reading—as they very well might. Dealing with this threat involves steps such as the following:

— Identify possible control variables related to the dependent variable.

— Get evidence about these variables.

— Demonstrate statistically and/or judgmentally that the groups do not differ on these control variables.

• When groups are used in a study of a treatment variable, they are labeled treatment (or experimental) and control groups. The treatment group gets the treatment; the control group does not get the treatment, but it does get a parallel, control activity. The groups must be equivalent on all subject variables related to the dependent variable and on all experiences except the treatment or the control activity. Otherwise, differences between the treatment and control groups on the dependent variable could not be attributed to the treatment. For example, suppose we were examining the effect of prereading activities on subsequent reading achievement in the primary grades. If the treatment and control subjects differed on some related variable, like intelligence level, the effects of the treatment could not be evaluated. Dealing with this threat involves procedures such as the following:

— Get a pool of subjects and assign them to the treatment and control groups by appropriate procedures (*e.g.*, van Dalen, 1973, pp. 274-279).

— Use statistical and judgmental evidence to demonstrate that the groups are equivalent on all variables which might affect the dependent variable.

Differential subject attrition. Attrition refers to the dropping out of subjects from the study. To maintain the study's integrity, this dropping out must be random. The subjects must not all have a particular characteristic. If the dropouts have a particular characteristic, like low interest in reading, the attrition could influence the dependent variable. The reason is that subjects remaining in the study might then have different characteristics than the original subjects identified for study. For example, suppose we were studying long-term growth in vocabulary. Over the years, we could lose a number of socially disadvantaged pupils who might come from non-homeowning families who tend to move more often. Because of a number of factors in their backgrounds, such pupils also probably show slower vocabulary growth. Loss of these pupils could lead to a biased growth curve for vocabulary; that is, the curve might reflect the growth only of more privileged pupils. Among procedures for dealing with differential subject attrition as a threat are:

- Choose subjects who can be expected to be more stable over time, carefully describing the characteristics of those subjects and limiting generalizations to subjects who have those characteristics.
- Keep records about the characteristics of the dropouts on all variables related to the dependent variable. By judgmental and statistical analyses show that the characteristics of the group do not change with time. Or, if the group's characteristics change, describe those characteristics and limit generalizations to populations who have those characteristics.

Selection interacting with other variables. When groups are used, selection may interact with all of the above threats to validity. That is, in contrast to the other groups, one group may experience a different history, show different psychological changes, respond differently to the testing, react differently to changes to tests, manifest a different form of statistical regression, or have a different amount of attrition. For example, let's look at differential attrition. Suppose, we were investigating the role of intelligence in growth in word-meaning skills and comprehension and interpretation skills. One approach could involve our studying intellectually retarded adolescents and intellectually normal adolescents. If, during the study, the more intelligent retarded subjects left school to go into vocational training programs, the less intelligent retarded subjects would be left in the study. In this case, differences in the reading skills between retarded and normal subjects might be spuriously larger than might exist in the population. Dealing with selection interacting with other threats involves procedures like the following:

- Use in exactly the same way for each group the procedures cited above for dealing with history, psychological changes, response to testing, changes in tests, statistical regression, and attrition equating groups on subject characteristics and all experiences which could influence the dependent variable.
- Collect and present evidence that the groups do not differ on any of these threats to validity. If they do differ, describe how and limit generalizations accordingly.

Conclusion. To repeat: When we interpret longitudinal research in reading, we should consider rival hypotheses about variables like the above threats to validity and identify whether they are plausible. If we can present reasons for rejecting these rival hypotheses, we can ascribe changes in the dependent variable to the particular variables we used as independent variables in the study. However, rejection of these rival hypotheses is difficult. We could get discouraged but we should not. Realistically, about the most we can ask of ourselves and others is that we design reasonably clean research and then limit generalizations systematically and explicitly by showing which of these rival hypotheses might have operated. Campbell and Stanley (1963) said it well:

> The average student or potential researcher reading [about the threats to validity] probably ends up with more things to worry about in designing an experiment than he had in mind to begin with. This is all to the good if it leads to the design and execution of better experiments and to more circumspection in drawing inferences from results. It is, however, an unwanted side effect if it creates a feeling of hopelessness with regard to achieving experimental control and leads to the abandonment of such efforts in favor of even more informal methods of investigation. Further, this formidable list of sources of invalidity might, with even more likelihood, reduce willingness to undertake designs in which from the very outset it can be seen that full control is lacking. Such an effect would be the opposite of what is intended.
>
> From the standpoint of the final interpretation of an experiment and the attempt to fit it into the developing science, every experiment is imperfect. What a check list of validity criteria can do is to make an experimenter more aware of the residual imperfections in his design so that on the relevant points he can be aware of competing interpretations of his data. He should, of course, design the very best experiment which the situation makes possible. He should deliberately seek out those artificial and natural laboratories which provide the best opportunities for control. But beyond that he should go ahead with experiment and interpretation, fully aware of the points of which the results are equivocal [p. 204].

Designs for studying changes with time

Research designs for longitudinal studies can be a bit elaborate and complex. In this section and the next, some simplified illustrations are presented for the research questions presented earlier. Control variables are not considered here because they differ depending on the nature of the problem. In the presentation of designs, elipsis (. . .) is used to show that material exists but is omitted for convenience. Analysis of variance procedures are used in the description of data processing. This choice was for ease in presentation. In actual situations, the nature of the particular problem, the data, or the situation might make more appropriate one of the other statistical procedures alluded to above.

Questions about changes with time pertain to how pupils' behavior changes with organic and physiological development accompanying age or how their behavior changes as they participate in common environmental experiences, like schooling, over time.

The Time Design

Does pupil behavior change over a period of time? The independent variable here is time. The dependent variable is the behavior which is being examined for the influence of time's concomitants. To answer the question, the beginning time, time periods, and the ending time to be worked with are specified. So is the measurement to be used to sample the dependent variable. A measurement is made at the beginning time and at each succeeding time period. Each measurement is made with the same or equivalent procedures. The design can be diagramed as in Figure 2.

First Time	Second Time	Third Time	....	Final Time
Measurement #1	Measurement #2	Measurement #3	....	Final Measurement

Figure 2. Time

With this design, plans should be made to deal with five possible threats to internal validity which would lead to rival hypotheses in interpretation; these are history, psychological changes, response to testing, changes in tests, and differential subject attrition.

The data obtained in this design may be processed with an analysis of variance model suitable for repeated measures. The summary table for the analysis would look like Table 1.

Table 1.

Source of Variation	df	Sum of Squares	Mean Square	F
Total	N-1	SS_{Ti}		
Time	t-1	SS_{Ti}	MS_T	MS_{Ti}/MS_{TiS}
Subjects	s-1	SS_S	MS_S	
Time x Subjects	(a-1) (s-1)	SS_{TiS}	MS_{TiS}	

The research question was: Does pupil behavior change over a period of time? The answer is in the F-ratio associated with time. If the F were not significant, we could infer that a change in behavior did not take place over the time period. If the F were significant, we could infer that a change of behavior did occur with time. Then, we could go on to analyze the nature of the trend, to see if it were linear, quadratic, and so on.

In interpretation, we would weigh an hypothesis about the effect of the independent variable, time, against rival hypotheses about history, psychological changes, response to testing, changes in tests, and differential subject attrition. If we could reject these rival hypotheses, then given significant statistics we could infer that the changes in the dependent variable are attributable to the physical, mental, and/or experiential changes which occur with time.

An example of the time question specified in reading is: In the elementary school years, what is the pattern and level of attainment in sight vocabulary growth? The research design would involve sampling pupils' sight vocabulary at Grade 1 and in subsequent years, at Grade 2, Grade 3, Grade 4, and so on.

The Time x Groups Design

Do different groups of pupils show different patterns of behavior change over a period of time? The independent variables are time and whatever variable is used in defining groups. To answer the question, the groups are identified. These groups are different on their defining characteristics and the same or equivalent on all characteristics and experiences related to the dependent variable. Then the *Time Design* is used in exactly the same way with each group. Figure 3 shows the diagram.

TIME

		First Time	Second Time	Third Time	...	Final Time
Group	Group 1	Measurement #1	Measurement #2	Measurement #3	...	Final Measurement
	Group 2	Measurement #1	Measurement #2	Measurement #3	...	Final Measurement

Figure 3. Time.

With this design, the threats to internal validity to be planned for are history and all of the other threats either affecting both groups the same way or operating in interaction with selection.

The data could be processed by analysis of variance model suitable for one independent variable and for one variable involving repeated measures. The summary for the analysis is shown in Table 2.

The research question was: Do different groups of pupils show different patterns of change over a period of time? We look first for the answer to the research question in the F ratio associated with the Time x Groups interaction. If it were significant, we could infer that the groups showed different patterns of behavior change with time. Then, we would go on to analyze the shape of each group's curve. For example, one group might show a faster rate of growth than another; one group might show a linear trend indicating a straight line development while another might

Table 2.

Source of Variation	df	Sum of Squares	Main Squares	F
Total	$t(n-1)$	SS_{To}		
Between Subjects	$N-1$	SS_{bS}		
Groups	$g-1$	SS_G	MS_G	$MS_G/MS_{E(b)}$
error (b)	$N-g$	$SS_{E(b)}$	$MS_{E(b)}$	
Within Subjects	$N(Ti-1)$	SS_{wS}		
Time	$ti-1$	SS_{Ti}	MS_{Ti}	$MS_{Ti}/MS_{E(w)}$
Time x Groups	$(ti-1)(g-1)$	SS_{TiG}	MS_{TiG}	$MS_{TiG}/MS_{E(w)}$
error (w)	$(ti-1)(N-g)$	$SS_{E(w)}$	$MS_{E(w)}$	

show a quadratic trend indicating growth followed by a plateau or vice versa. There are several possibilities for such differential patterns.

If the Time x Groups interaction were not significant, then we would look at the effects of Groups alone and Time alone.

- If both the Time effect and the Groups effect were significant, then we could infer that the groups differed in level of response, that change with time occurred, and that the groups showed the same pattern of change with time. Then, we would go on to examine the nature of the difference between the groups and the nature of the change with time that both showed.
- If the Time effect were significant and the Groups effect were not, then we could infer that the groups did not differ in level of response, that change with time occurred, and that both groups showed the same pattern of change with time.
- If the Time effect were not significant and the Groups effect were, then we could infer that the groups differed in level of response but that they did not show a change over time. Then, we would go on to examine the between groups difference.
- If neither the Time effect nor the Groups effect were significant, then we would infer that the groups did not differ in level of response and that they did not show a change in behavior with time.

In interpretation, we would need to weigh hypotheses about the effects of the independent variables, time and the grouping variable, against the rival hypotheses about the several threats to validity singly and in interaction with selection. If we could reject these rival hypotheses, then we could ascribe patterns and differences in dependent variable to the independent variables in a way consistent with the results of the analyses.

An example of a Time x Groups question with implications for reading is: Between the ages of two and six do intellectually retarded and intellectually normal pupils differ in the amount and pattern of change in the prefixes, inflectional suffixes, and derivational suffixes they use correctly in their oral language? Here retarded and normal pupils who are alike on characteristics and experiences related to language are identified. Then, measurements are made of their use of morphemes at CA2, and, in subsequent years, at CA3, CA4, CA5, and CA6.

Designs for studying changes with time and treatments

Questions about changes with time and treatments pertain to how pupils' behavior changes with some training procedure they participate in over time.

The Time x Treatment Design

Does a given treatment affect pupil behavior over a period of time? The independent variables are time and treatment. The dependent variable is the behavior examined for the influence of time and the treatment. The pool of subjects is subdivided into equated treatment and control groups. Given the treatment and control groups, the Time Design is used exactly the same way with the two groups. In addition, the treatment group is given the treatment; the control group is given the parallel activity. These treatment and control activities are started *after* one or more initial measurements are taken. The diagram is shown in Figure 4.

		First Time	Second Time	Third Time	... Final Time
Treatment	Treatment Group		(Treatment throughout the time period starting after Measurement #1)		
		Measurement #1	Measurement #2	Measurement #3	Final ... Measurement
	Control Group		(Control activity throughout the time period starting after Measurement #1)		
		Measurement #1	Measurement #2	Measurement #3	Final ... Measurement

Figure 4. Time

In this design, plans need to be made to deal with all of the threats to internal validity, singly and in interaction with selection, that is, history, psychological changes, response to testing, and so on.

Conducting longitudinal research

The data could be processed by an analysis of variance model with provision for one independent variable and one repeated measure. The summary is shown in Table 3.

Table 3.

Source of Variation	df	Sum of Squares	Mean Squares	F
Total	$ti(N-1)$	SS_{To}		
Between Subjects	$N-1$	SS_{bS}		
Treatment	$tr-1$	SS_{Tr}	MS_{Tr}	MS_{Tr}/MS_{Eb}
error (b)	$N-tr$	$SS_{E(b)}$	$MS_{E(b)}$	
Within Subjects	$N(ti-1)$	SS_{wS}		
Time	$ti-1$	SS_{Ti}	MS_{Ti}	$MS_{Ti}/MS_{E(w)}$
Time x Treatment	$(ti-1)(tr-1)$	SS_{TiTr}	MS_{TiTr}	$MS_{TiTr}/MS_{E(w)}$
error (w)	$(ti-1)(N-tr)$	$SS_{E(w)}$	$MS_{E(w)}$	

The research question was: Does a given treatment affect pupil behavior over a period of time? The evidence for the question starts with the F ratio for the Time x Treatment interaction. If the Time x Treatment F ratio were significant, we would infer that the treatment group and the control group showed different patterns of change as time passed. The control group would show the change accompanying time alone and common experiences. The treatment group would show the additional change accompanying the treatment. Next, we would go on to describe the nature of the change, whether it was equal increments, increments increasing in size, or increments decreasing in size.

If the Time x Treatment interaction were not significant, there are several possibilities.

- If both the Time F ratio and the Treatment F ratio were significant, then we could infer that both Treatment and Control groups showed the same pattern of change with time even though they operated at different levels of attainment. Next, we would go on to examine whether the difference between the treatment and control groups were in the expected direction, that is, if the treatment had the effect anticipated.

- If the Time F ratio were significant and the Treatment F ratio were not, we would infer that the treatment had no effect and that all subjects showed a change with time.

- If the Time F ratio were not significant and the Treatment F ratio were, we would infer that the subjects did not change over time but that the groups differed. Next, we would go on to examine if the treatment had the expected effect, that is, if the treatment was effective.

- If neither the Time F ratio nor the Treatment F ratio were significant, then we would infer that the treatment did not have an effect and that behavior did not change with time.

In interpretation, we would weigh hypotheses about the independent variables, time and treatments, and rival hypotheses about the threats to internal validity singly and in interaction with selection. If we could rule out the rival hypotheses, we could attribute patterns and differences in the dependent variable to the independent variables in a way consistent with the results of the analyses.

An example of the Time x Treatment question in reading is: In terms of phonics skills, what pattern and level of attainment do pupils show if the phonics program in their basal readers is supplemented by a phonics program like the Phonovisual materials in the primary grades? The research design would involve identifying treatment subjects and control subjects who are similar on all characteristics and experiences related to phonics. Their facility in dealing with the various aspects of the vowel and consonant sounds would be measured at the beginning of the first, second, third, and fourth grades. Treatment subjects would be taught with a basal reader program and the Phonovisual program. Control subjects would be taught with the same basal reader program. In the time allotted to the Phonovisual program in the Treatment group, they would be given a parallel activity.

The Time x Treatments x Groups Design

Do different groups respond differently to a given treatment over a period of time? The independent variables are time, the defining characteristics for groups, and the treatment. The dependent variable is the behavior studied for influence. The design is a combination of the Time x Treatments Design and the Time x Groups Design. In summary: The groups are identified so that they are different on the defining characteristics and equivalent on all other variables and experiences related to the dependent variable. The groups are subdivided into treatment and control subgroups in a way that they are equivalent on all variables related to the dependent variable. The treatment is specified. So is the control activity. The measure to sample the dependent variable is identified. The beginning time, time periods, and final time are chosen. The treatments are given to the treatment subgroups over the time period, the control activities to the control subgroups. The same measurements are taken at the same time on all subjects. The design is shown in Figure 5.

In this design, all of the threats to internal validity could operate singly and in combination with selection. Plans need to be made to cir-

		First Time	Second Time	Third Time	... Final Time
Group 1	Treatment Subgroup	(Treatment throughout the time period starting after Measurement #1)			
		Measurement #1	Measurement #2	Measurement #3	... Final Measurement
	Control Subgroup	(Control activity through the time period starting after Measurement #1)			
		Measurement #1	Measurement #2	Measurement #3	... Final Measurement
Group 2	Treatment Subgroup	(Treatment throughout the time period starting after Measurement #1)			
		Measurement #1	Measurement #2	Measurement #3	... Final Measurement
	Control Subgroup	(Control activity throughout the time period starting after Measurement #1)			
		Measurement #1	Measurement #2	Measurement #3	... Final Measurement

Figure 5.   Time

cumvent these threats or, if that is impossible, to get information about the extent they operate.

The data could be processed with an analysis of variance model with the provision for two independent variables and one repeated measure. The summary is shown in Table 4.

The research question was: Do different groups respond differently to a given treatment over a period of time? The research question would begin to be answered by the F ratio for Time x Groups x Treatment interaction. If it were significant, we would infer that the groups responded differently to the treatment as time passed. Then, we would go on to explore the nature of this differential response. There could be many patterns. For example, one group might show a steady benefit over the time span while the other might show an initial benefit followed by a leveling off, and so on.

If the Time x Groups x Treatment interaction F ratio were not significant, we could infer that the groups showed a similar response to the treatments as time passed. Then, we would go on to explore the nature of this similar response. First, we would examine the Time x Groups interaction and the Time x Treatment interaction as described above with their respective designs. If these interactions were not significant, we would look at the influence of Time as described above with the Time Design while looking at the Between Subjects effects.

Table 4.

Source of Variation	df	Sum of Squares	Mean Squares	F
Total	(ti) (g) (tr) (n)-1	SS_{To}		
Between Subjects	(g) (tr) (n)-1	SS_{bS}	MS_{bS}	
Groups	g-1	SS_G	MS_G	$MS_G/MS_{E(b)}$
Treatments	tr-1	SS_{Tr}	MS_{Tr}	$MS_{Tr}/MS_{E(b)}$
Groups x Treatment	(g-1) (tr-1)	SS_{GTr}	MS_{GTr}	$MS_{GTr}/MS_{E(b)}$
Error (b)	(g) (tr) (n-1)	$SS_{E(b)}$	$MS_{E(b)}$	
Within Subjects	(g) (tr) (n) (ti-1)	SS_{wS}		
Time	ti-1	SS_{Ti}	MS_{Ti}	$MS_{Ti}/MS_{E(w)}$
Time x Groups	(ti-1) (g-1)	SS_{TiG}	MS_{TiG}	$MS_{TiG}/MS_{E(w)}$
Time x Treatment	(ti-1) (tr-1)	SS_{TiTr}	MS_{TiTr}	$MS_{TiTr}/MS_{E(w)}$
Time x Groups x Treatment	(ti-1) (g-1) (tr-1)	SS_{TiGTr}	MS_{TiGTr}	$MS_{TiGTr}/MS_{E(w)}$
Error (w)	(g) (tr) (ti-1) (n-1)	$SS_{E(w)}$	$MS_{E(w)}$	

- If the Time main effect and the Groups x Treatment interaction effect were significant, we would infer that the groups reacted differentially to the treatment with one showing a greater difference over its control group than the other and that this differential difference continued over the time period studied.
- If the Time, Groups, and Treatments main effects were significant and the Groups x Treatment interaction effect were not, then we could infer that the Treatment had an influence and that this influence was similar for both groups over the time span.
- If only the Time and Groups main effects or only the Time and Treatment main effects were significant, then we would interpret them as we did the main effects in the Time x Group design and the Time x Treatment designs, respectively.

In interpretation, we would weigh hypotheses about the time, treatments, and groups independent variables against the rival hypotheses about history, and so on. If the rival hypotheses could be discounted, then we could ascribe the changes in the dependent variable to the independent variables in a way consistent with the results of the analyses.

An example of the Time x Treatment x Groups question in reading is: In terms of comprehension and interpretation skills, do pupils from non-English speaking backgrounds and pupils from English speaking backgrounds respond differently to supplementing their basal reading program with a prose listening program over the elementary school years? The research design would involve identifying pupils from an English speaking background and a non-English speaking background and subdividing them into treatment and control subgroups. These groups and subgroups would be equivalent on variables and experiences related to learning the comprehension and interpretation skills. At the same time, the dependent variables, the comprehension and interpretation skills to be studied, would be specified and methods of measurement identified. The treatment subgroups would be given the supplementary listening program. In the same time period, the control subgroups would be given a parallel activity. The measurements would be administered in the same way to all subjects at the beginning of grades 1, 2, 3, 4, 5, 6, and 7.

Extensions

We have looked at only a few aspects of longitudinal research. The following points should be noted very carefully:

- The questions and designs we have considered are very uncomplex ones. Longitudinal research can, and usually does, involve measures of more than one dependent variable, more than one independent subject variable, more than one treatment variable, more than one set of groups, more than one set of treatments, and so on. Also, it can involve various procedures for identifying subjects and forming groups. It can involve various approaches to defining and specifying the independent variables and sampling the dependent variables.
- We have alluded only obliquely to psychometric and statistical problems in longitudinal, or more strictly time series, research. They can be formidable.
- We did not consider logistics at all. Keeping up with a set of subjects over an extended time period involves effort devoted to logistics in addition to the logistical efforts required for other kinds of research.
- We started with questions as given and focused on methodology. We did not discuss the origin of longitudinal research questions, as with all other research questions, in theory or in other rational bases. That is, the questions and expectations posed must follow from some set of guiding principles from substantive concerns in reading pedagogy, child psychology, learning, sociology, and so on.

Conducting and evaluating longitudinal research requires knowledge about these matters. This knowledge can be acquired in courses in substantive areas and research methodology, apprenticeship in on-going longitudinal studies, and reference works like Annastasi (1968), Best (1970), Cronbach (1970), Edwards (1968), Harris (1963), Travers (1969, 1973), and Weiner (1971).

REFERENCES

ANNASTASI, ANNE. *Psychological testing* (3rd ed.) New York: Macmillan, 1968.

BAYLEY, NANCY. Learning in adulthood: The role of intelligence. In Herbert J. Klausmeier and Chester W. Harris (Eds.) *Analyses of concept learning.* New York: Academic Press, 1966. Pp. 117-138.

BAYLEY, NANCY. Behavioral correlates of mental growth: Birth to 36 years. *American Psychologist,* 1968, *23,* 1-17.

BAYLEY, NANCY. Development of mental abilities. In Paul H. Mussen (Ed.) *Carmichael's manual of child psychology,* Vol. 1. New York: Wiley, 1970. Pp. 1163-1209.

BEREITER, CARL. Some persisting dilemmas in the measurement of change. In C. W. Harris (Ed.) *Problems in measuring change.* Madison: University of Wisconsin Press, 1963. Pp. 3-20.

BEST, JOHN W. *Research in education* (2d ed.) Englewood Cliffs, N.J.: Prentice-Hall, 1970.

BOND, GUY L., & DYKSTRA, ROBERT. *Coordinating center for first grade reading instruction programs.* Final Report, Project No. X-001: Contract No. OE-5-10-264, February, 1967. U.S. Department of Health, Education, and Welfare.

BRACHT, GLENN H., & GLASS, GENE V. The external validity of experiments. *American Education Research Journal,* 1968, 5, 437-474.

BRUININKS, ROBERT H., & LUCKER, WILLIAM G. *Change and stability in correlations between intelligence and reading test scores among disadvantaged children.* 1974. (ERIC Document Reproduction Service No. ED 083 346)

CAMPBELL, DONALD T. From description to experimentation: Interpreting trends as quasi-experiments. In Chester W. Harris (Ed.) *Problems in measuring change.* Madison: University of Wisconsin Press, 1963, 212-242.

CAMPBELL, DONALD T., & STANLEY, JULIAN C. Experimental and quasi-experimental designs in research on teaching. In Nate L. Gage (Ed.), *Handbook of research on teaching.* Chicago: Rand McNally, 1963. Pp. 171-246.

CRONBACH, LEE J. *Essential of psychological testing* (3d ed.) New York: Harper & Row, 1970.

DYKSTRA, ROBERT. *Continuation of the coordinating center for first grade reading instruction programs.* Final Report, Project No. X-001: Contract No. OE-5-10-264, 1967. U.S. Department of Health, Education, and Welfare.

EDWARDS, ALLEN L. *Experimental design in psychological research.* (3d ed.) New York: Holt, Rinehart, and Winston, 1968.

HARRIS, C. W. (Ed.) *Problems in measuring change.* Madison: University of Wisconsin Press, 1963. Pp. 212-242.

MAZURKIEWICZ, ALBERT J. *The early to read–i.t.a. program: Effects and aftermath. A six year longitudinal study.* 1972. (ERIC Document Reproduction Service No. ED 059 850)

SATZ, PAUL. *Some predictive antecedents of specific reading disability: A two, three and four-year follow-up.* 1975. (ERIC Document Reproduction Service No. ED 101 298)

STONE, A. A., & ONQUE, GLORIA C. *Longitudinal studies of child personality.* Cambridge: Harvard University Press, 1959.

TRAVERS, ROBERT M. W. *An introduction to educational research.* (3d ed.) New York: Macmillan, 1969.

TRAVERS, ROBERT M. W. *Second handbook of research on teaching.* Chicago: Rand McNally, 1973.

VAN DALEN, DEOBOLD B. *Understanding educational research: An introduction* (3d ed.) New York: McGraw-Hill, 1973.

WEINER, BENJAMIN J. *Statistical principles in experimental design.* (2d ed.) New York: McGraw-Hill, 1971.

Interpreting the findings: some cautions

ALBERT J. HARRIS, Emeritus
City University of New York

The careful shopper in today's continuing inflation cannot always get the best possible value for his money, but he can, if he wishes, subscribe to *Consumer's Report* and be guided by the results of impartial tests of competing products, such as cars, electrical appliances, and cameras. The U.S. Bureau of Standards and the Food and Drug Administration set minimum quality standards for a wide variety of products. We are protected by various governmental agencies against dangerous or ineffective drugs, noxious pesticides, and contaminated food.

But no agency protects the educational consumer from practices that are based on shoddy research, or on tradition unsupported by research, or from innovative practices that receive sensational widespread publicity on little other than unsubstantiated claims. The recommendations of hundreds of professors, the curriculum guides used in thousands of schools, the plans of hundreds of thousands of teachers, and the lives of millions of children can be and have been profoundly influenced by particular research studies. As David Russell (1961) pointed out, some reading research has made a real impact on reading instruction; and as Harry Singer showed (1970), some good reading research has not had the influence on practice that it deserved, while other studies have influenced practice far beyond what was warranted.

The importance of reading the full report

The research literature related to reading is now so voluminous that no single individual can read it all. The wise consumer of reading research does not attempt to be omnivorous. It is no longer possible for a William S. Gray to personally summarize and review the entire field each year. Even when the task is shared by four people and their assistants, as in the recent annual summaries in the *Reading Research Quarterly,* the job is arduous.

One is tempted, therefore, to rely on brief abstracts and summaries. The annual summary in *Reading Research Quarterly, Psychological Abstracts,* and the ERIC system's *Research in Education* provide abstracts that indicate what a study was about and often give the main conclusions. These abstracts are non-evaluative and usually do not provide enough information to allow the reader to judge the validity of the results and conclusions. The abstracts of doctoral dissertations published in *Dissertation Abstracts* are more variable. Some of them contain enough detail to allow a fairly adequate evaluation. Others are so uninformative that one is tempted to ignore the study on the grounds that if the author couldn't write a better abstract, many flaws would be present in his dissertation.

The proper use of an abstract is to provide a full citation and enough information to judge if the paper is relevant to the topic one is investigating. If it is relevant, one should try to find and read the report.

There is a similar relationship between a brief journal article which summarizes a long unpublished report, and the full report. A case in point is the *Cooperative First Grade Studies.* Most people who are acquainted with the results have relied on the summaries printed in *The Reading Teacher.* A smaller number have read the reports of the Coordinating Center (Bond and Dykstra, 1967; Dykstra, 1968) which were published in *Reading Research Quarterly.* Even for the director of one of the 27 studies, wading through the full reports of the other 26 projects was an onerous task. Yet only in that way could one get at the fine points of methodology, statistical method, and logical inference or could one judge the effects of the many compromises with ideal research design that had to be made because of circumstances in the schools.

Is the study centered on one or more clear and testable hypotheses?

This issue has been discussed in other papers in this collection, particularly by Dr. Wardrop, and will not be dwelt on here. In research, an hypothesis is tenable until it is disproved. It is up to the researcher to determine if the null hypothesis holds or not, with regard to particular effects or differences. The finding of a statistically significant difference or effect does not establish the variable or hypothesis in which the researcher is interested as the cause of that difference. Narrowing the possibilities down to one may require setting up and testing a number of alternative hypotheses.

Cautions in interpreting findings

Does the researcher seem to have been impartial?

Most reading research is conducted by people who are not known to have a personal stake in the outcome. When reading a report involving the evaluation of a procedure which the report author has devised, or to which he is known to be quite favorably inclined, the reader should read with greater than usual caution.

Let us assume that five comparisons of a particular beginning reading program with other programs have been completed. Two projects report significant differences in favor of the new procedure, while three do not. The two projects with favorable results were conducted by the coauthors of the procedure, while the three other projects were conducted by people with no obvious stake in the outcome. Under such circumstances, one is justified in concluding that the favorable results obtained by the coauthors are probably not generalizable to other staffs and pupil populations.

It is not necessary to assume any intentional dishonesty or doctoring of results. In testing the value of a new medicine, it has been shown over and over that if the people who administer the drugs know which patients get the new drug and which get a control pill, that awareness by itself can bias the results. Valid results in such studies require the use of a double-blind procedure, in which the medical staff as well as the patients do not know which patients get the real drug. Otherwise, subtle differences in manner seem to provide a stronger suggestion of cure to those receiving the new drug and this influences the results.

If an educational researcher has a strong bias in favor of one of the variables being compared, this bias is likely to exert influence on participating teachers despite honest efforts to carry on the study in an impartial manner. The teachers using that variable may feel that they are on the researcher's side, and they may exert extra effort. Teachers in contrasted variables are less likely to exert similar effort, since favorable results for their variable will be a disappointment for the project director. Research assistants have even been known, in a few cases, to have falsified results so as to get them to agree with the project director's expectations.

Unless there is evidence of biased procedure, the careful reader accepts the results of such a study as valid for the particular population of teachers and pupils. Caution requires questioning the degree to which similar results are obtainable with other teachers and pupils, in situations in which a neutral, objective attitude about the variable may be assumed.

Sometimes an experimenter reports results in which his admittedly preferred variable fails to show any advantage. This certainly testifies to a strong effort to be objective. On the other hand, it does not eliminate the possibility that under truly impartial conditions, there might have been a significant difference against that variable. Replication by other investigators with other populations is the only real protection against possibly biased results.

Are the variables clearly and adequately described?

Educational research reports are frequently restricted in length by the policies of the journals to which they are submitted. Often a project on which the full report ran to as many as 300 pages has been briefly summarized in an article of four to eight pages. In such a summary, it is usually impossible to do much more than present the issues and the major results. The reader often finds a general and more or less vague description of the experimental variables. Control variables are less likely to be adequately described than new or experimental variables. Often a control variable is described in a single sentence which states that this consisted of the usual procedure, leaving the reader to conjecture what that "usual" procedure really was. There may actually have been no "usual" procedure if each control teacher was free to teach as he or she pleased. Rather there may have been a hodge-podge of varying procedures.

When there is no description of a control variable, or a very inadequate description, one has to wonder also about the possibility of a strong Hawthorne Effect. The researcher who does not bother to describe what the control teachers did may not have bothered to find out, let alone to provide direction, training, and motivation comparable to that given the experimental teachers.

If an unsatisfyingly brief journal article is important to the reader, it may be necessary to locate the full unpublished report and to look for more complete presentation of essential details there. The ERIC system provides access to thousands of unpublished reports. Complete dissertations may be obtained through University Microfilms. Ideally the full report should describe each variable in sufficient detail to allow another researcher to replicate the study. An unclear or inadequate description of a variable raises the suspicion that a similar lack of precision characterized the operation of that variable in the study. If the reader cannot find the information he wants in the report, a personal letter to the author usually elicits a polite and cooperative response.

Are the variables potentially powerful?

As any reader of educational research knows, the most frequently reported finding is a lack of statistically significant differences. It is actually unusual to find a set of results showing a consistent, significant, and unequivocal difference in favor of one of the variables. Rather than agree with some skeptics that it doesn't really matter what teachers do, one should inquire whether or not the variables being compared were

Cautions in interpreting findings

sufficiently different and sufficiently powerful to have a reasonable chance to produce different results.

A researcher who is interested in determining the effects of a particular kind of intervention often finds it easy to assume that if the only change made in the education of the subjects is the introduction of that intervention, the intervention is the effective determiner of pupil performance on the criterion measures. But let us consider a fairly typical example. The researcher is interested in finding out the usefulness of a series of 20 lessons, of about a half hour each, intended to improve ability to comprehend and follow printed directions. The lessons are written at a fourth reader level and are used with two classes of fourth graders, while two other classes, equated with these in mean IQ and reading level, read similar materials without specific guidance in following directions. A special test of ability to read to follow directions is used as a pretest with an alternate form as a posttest. Can a difference be reasonably expected?

Here are some of the possible sources of weakness in the experimental variable:

- All of the pupils may have had some instructional guidance in following directions in previous grades, making the experimental lessons just a small addition to one group's previous instruction.

- The total instructional time for the experimental variable was 20 half-hour lessons, or 10 hours. Reading of textbooks in mathematics, spelling, and so forth may have involved an average of 15 minutes a day following directions, which in 20 weeks would amount to about 25 hours of unguided practice, not counting similar practice in previous grades. Thus the experimental group may have received 10 hours of guided practice and 20 plus hours of unguided practice, while the control group received 30 plus hours of unguided practice. It would be surprising if the 20 lessons produced much of a difference.

- The above estimates of time spent in unguided practice do not allow for some corrective guidance in reading number problems and other guidance in reading directions during periods not labeled as reading instruction. They also do not include practice at home while assembling models, baking cookies, working for Scout merit badges, and so forth.

It seems evident that a study like this does not contrast training in a particular skill with no training, but rather a little more guided practice with a little more unguided practice. The difference in variables is probably not great enough to produce any real difference in results, even if a completely valid criterion measure were available. Many studies reporting no significant differences have been exercises in futility because the researcher failed to create enough difference between the experimental variable and the opportunities for learning in the rest of the pupils' lives.

Have appropriate experimental controls been used?

In a paper of this length, it is impossible to go into any detail about the many kinds of errors which an unwary or unsophisticated research designer may unintentionally commit. The long chapter by Campbell and Stanley (1963) in the *Handbook of Research on Teaching* deserves intensive study by anyone who wants to be an informed evaluator of educational experimental studies. To me their discussion was invaluable and I have reread parts of it again and again.

Aside from the adequacy of formal experimental design, the alert reader should look for indications that the dice may have been loaded, deliberately or through unintentional error, so as to favor one variable.

Such favoritism can take many forms. One is allowing contrasted groups that were equated at the beginning of the study to become un-equated before the end of the study. In one of the Cooperative First Grade Studies that was continued beyond the first year, one variable lost 20 percent of its pupil population through non-promotion at the end of the first grade, while another variable lost only 6 percent. It is not surprising that the former variable came out ahead of the latter on second grade posttests. Even if the groups were re-equated on original pretest scores, the presence of 14 percent more slow learners in one set of classrooms may have influenced the teachers in that variable to slow down the instructional pace, which would have reduced opportunities to make superior scores.

A second source of possible bias lies in the assignment of teachers. If teacher volunteers are assigned to a new method, while teachers from the non-volunteer group are assigned to control classes, that in itself should raise a suspicion that teacher ability and enthusiasm were not evenly balanced.

A third problem arises when the variables operate in different schools or in different school districts. This is often the case in studies which draw comparisons between methods which have been employed in their respective schools for several years. In the Cooperative First Grade Studies it was found that equating populations for measured pupil abilities and teacher characteristics was not sufficient; some schools and districts had high scores regardless of method used, and others had low scores regardless of method used; and this was true after an attempt to control for pupil abilities by using a covariance procedure (Bond and Dykstra, 1967; Dykstra, 1968). Thus it was possible to attribute differences found to the experimental variables only when the contrasting methods operated in the same schools and districts.

A related problem is the unknown and usually unmeasurable influence of the attitudes and behaviors of administrators, supervisors, and teachers not involved in the study. These may range from supportive and cooperative to obstructionistic and antagonistic. Rarely can one find mention of these possible influences in a research report. Yet those who have conducted research in the real world setting of the schools know that the benevolent neutrality which is generally assumed does not always exist. This can be a most important source of error, despite the fact that it is rarely mentioned or discussed.

Are the measurement procedures used valid for the purposes of the study?

One of the central problems in reading research is the selection of tests or other measurement procedures which are used to measure the results. The reliability of educational and psychological tests of various kinds is relatively easy to establish. Test validity is not a constant but varies according to the many situations in which a particular test may be used. If one is trying to gauge the value of instruction in syllabication, it makes a difference whether the test of syllabication employed requires just counting the number of syllables in a word, drawing lines to show where syllables begin and end, or stating and applying syllabication rules. If one is trying to find out the effect of syllabication skill on word recognition, a test of oral pronunciation of words in a list may give quite different results from a vocabulary test in multiple choice form. So the results obtained are sometimes predetermined by the criterion measures selected.

Standardized reading tests, often used as pretests and posttests, have come under severe criticism in recent years. Criterion-based tests often have more apparent face validity, but may be low in reliability and may employ arbitrary pass-fail standards. Ratings and self-report questionnaires have their own limitations. The careful reader tries to decide for himself whether the choice of measures used in a study was reasonable and relevant to the problem.

An inadequate criterion measure can lead investigators up blind alleys for years. For example, many studies of lateral dominance and reading have used only two categories for handedness, left and right. Subjects who seemed intermediate in handedness were forced into the left or right category, and relationships to reading were usually found to be non-significant. Those studies which employed a third category of mixed or incomplete handedness were more likely to find significantly poorer reading in the mixed handedness group than in those with established handedness (Harris, 1957; Cohen and Glass, 1968).

Is the statistical treatment appropriate?

If one is not familiar with the merits, limitations, and requirements for the many different kinds of statistical procedures used in educational research, one has to assume that the researcher had sought competent statistical advice and leave it to statistical experts to argue whether or not the procedures used were the best that could have been employed.

One of the important differences between laboratory experimentation and classroom learning is that children in classrooms are usually taught in groups. When the same procedure is used simultaneously with all members of a group or a class, the group or class should be the statistical unit in statistical analysis. If four classrooms are used for each variable, and each class is taught as a group, the number of cases for tests of statistical significance is properly four classes rather than 100 pupils. With an N of four, a substantial difference is needed to satisfy tests of statistical significance; with an N of 100, a very small difference may look significant. The careful reader should note the author's choice of statistical unit and weigh the evidence of statistical significance accordingly.

A related concern is with the actual size and importance of differences found. There is a growing practice of reporting only whether or not a significant difference was found, without giving the statistical findings on which that conclusion is based. This is a very unsatisfactory practice in that it denies the reader the information he needs in order to check the author's conclusions. Somewhat better is the practice of giving results entirely in raw scores, so that a reader would have to locate a table of norms and look up the derived grade, stanine, or percentile scores in order to judge how important the difference was. Sometimes a statistically significant difference does not amount to much when translated into grade equivalents or other derived scores. A careful reader likes to find mean raw scores and derived scores, so he can judge the practical importance of the differences found.

Are the author's conclusions justified by his results?

In reading the section of discussion and conclusions in a research report, one should keep three main questions in mind:

- Does the author provide a reasonable and logical explanation of the results obtained? Sometimes bias shows clearly in an attempt to make non-significant results look significant, or to argue away results which do not support the author's expectations. If objective test results are non-supportive, pupil and teacher expressions of satisfaction or dissatisfaction may be played up, or vice versa.
- Does the author focus on one possible explanation of his results and ignore other possible explanations that may be equally plausible? This may indicate a limited vision rather than a bias, but it still can mislead the reader. If there is just one reasonable explanation possible, the problem may be considered solved. If there are two or more interpretations possible, one looks for recognition of that fact, and for recommendation

Cautions in interpreting findings

for additional studies which might eliminate some of the alternatives. Putting all reasonable interpretations in the report, rather than just the one which the author happens to favor, is a desirable procedure not always followed.

- Is the degree to which the author generalizes from his results justified by the conditions of the project? At times we have been misled into accepting sweeping generalizations based on studies which utilized quite unrepresentative populations, settings, or both.

A notable example of generalization far beyond the data is the statement that a minimum mental age of 6 years, or sometimes 6½ years, is necessary for a child to be successful in beginning reading. Such statements were quite commonly found in books on reading instruction for about 30 years, from the 1930s into the 1960s. This notion, as Singer (1970) has pointed out, seems to have had its origins in a study by Morphett and Washburne (1931) which received wide attention because of Washburne's prestige as a leader and innovator in the Progressive Education movement. Morphett and Washburne actually recommended that ". . . a child would gain considerably in speed of learning if beginning reading was postponed until the child had attained a mental age of six years and six months" on the Detroit First Grade Intelligence Test. At that mental age, 78 percent had made satisfactory progress in reading, while below it, the percentage succeeding diminished. Note that they did not say that such a mental age was essential, but only that learning would proceed faster. The study had been conducted in Winnetka, Illinois, a suburban community in which the average IQ was quite high and whose schools were already pioneering in individualized instruction.

The many authorities who cited that study during the next 30 years as a basis for pronouncements about mental age and reading readiness ignored the unrepresentativeness of the school system, the instructional methods, the rather exactingly high standard for passing, and the abilities of the pupils, and tended to state that a minimum mental age was a requirement for success in beginning reading—a generalization which went well beyond the conclusions of the original researchers. It is quite possible that some of these writers never bothered to read the original report critically, but simply borrowed the citation and interpretation from a previous writer. Uncritical overgeneralization from unrepresentative research led to the unnecessary postponement of beginning reading instruction for millions of children.

What this all adds up to is that the consumer of educational research needs to utilize the skills of critical reading. He does not trust the decisions of editors on whether or not to publish a particular report. He is not willing to accept an author's conclusions at face value but applies his own sophistication in research design, statistical analysis, and inferential reasoning. When he does this, he discovers that a perfectly designed and executed research study is as rare as a completely unflawed diamond. With an understanding of the constraints under which educational research is carried on, particularly in school-based research, he does not expect complete perfection. But he tries to be aware of the many factors which limit generalization from obtained results, and uses this awareness in deciding how far to trust the conclusions formulated by the researcher.

REFERENCES

BOND, GUY L., & DYKSTRA, ROBERT. The cooperative research program in first-grade reading. *Reading Research Quarterly,* Summer 1967, *2,* 5-126.
CAMPBELL, DONALD T., & STANLEY, JULIAN C. Experimental and quasi-experimental designs for research on teaching. In Gage, Nathan L. (Ed.) *Handbook of research on teaching.* Chicago: Rand McNally, 1963. Pp. 171-246.
COHEN, ALICE, & GLASS, GERALD G. Lateral dominance and reading ability. *The Reading Teacher,* 1968, *21,* 343-348.
DYKSTRA, ROBERT. Summary of the second-grade phase of the Cooperative Research Program in primary reading instruction. *Reading Research Quarterly,* 1968, *4,* 49-70.
HARRIS, ALBERT J. Lateral dominance, directional confusion, and reading disability. *Journal of Psychology,* 1957, *44,* 283-294.
MORPHETT, MABEL V., & WASHBURNE, CARLETON. When should children begin to read? *Elementary School Journal,* 1931, *31,* 496-503.
RUSSELL, DAVID H. Reading research that makes a difference. *Elementary English,* February 1961, *38,* 74-78.
SINGER, HARRY. Research that should have made a difference. *Elementary School Journal,* January 1970, *47,* 27-34.

Linguistics in reading research

RONALD WARDHAUGH
University of Toronto

Linguistics is important in reading research because serious thinking about language is necessary if we are to continue to obtain useful insights into language development and reading and any relationship that might exist between the two. However, it takes considerable effort to acquire linguistic sophistication: becoming proficient in linguistics is no easy task. A doctoral degree in linguistics takes an average of half a dozen years of graduate study and marks only a beginning level of competence for most recipients! Sophistication of almost any kind is all too often missing from the work that is done on language and reading, even though attempts are made to appear sophisticated. The principal attempt, of course, is to use current linguistic terminology in reporting on work in reading. Unfortunately, the attempt sometimes provides evidence that the researchers have stepped far outside their linguistic competence and understanding. It is, unfortunately, all too easy to recognize the garblings, the misunderstandings, and the nonsequiturs that characterize such endeavors. Terms are misused, concepts are confused, subtitles are overlooked, and strawmen are stuffed, beaten, and dispatched. Of course, the alternative is not to attempt to use any, or much, linguistic knowledge at all—and this alternative is much more common—and to produce the instant museum pieces of which the literature is so full. The real difficulty is finding the productive middleground—the area in which good linguistic knowledge can be used to bring forth a harvest worth gathering.

Linguistic knowledge must also be used cautiously in language and reading research. But it is not necessarily the case that better research would inevitably be done if sophisticated linguistic concepts were introduced wholesale into that research. On the contrary, the results of "going wild" about linguistics could well be disastrous. Lest these statements seem wildly contradictory to each other, let me provide some reasons for giving this warning about the sometimes "excessive" consumption of linguistics. Linguistics is not "unsafe at any speed"—rather it is unsafe at certain speeds, particularly at the speed at which one emphasis gives way to another.

The nature of linguistics

Linguists are concerned with theoretical issues having to do with what language in general is, about how individual languages are structured (for example, English), and about how languages change and vary over space and time. They deal in powerful abstractions and they tend to use evidence either to support or to deny claims rather than to deal with issues exhaustively. Consequently, linguists do not offer comprehensive statements about masses and masses of data: for example, they do not usually attempt to write long and exhaustive grammars; instead they offer tantalizing theories, generally of a very powerful nature with suggestions as to how these theories may be tested this way or that. Quite often one counter-example—that is, one piece of contradictory evidence—is more important than a hundred confirming examples for a linguist because the theory must be reformulated. It is this kind of sophisticated concern which is most respected in theoretical linguistics. The term *theory* does not appear to be used this way in research in reading.

There is, of course, another level of sophistication in linguistics— the level which takes concepts derived from what can be called "frontier" linguistics and deals with quantities of data in terms of those concepts. This is the level of the textbook presentation of linguistic ideas, a level which is inevitably characterized by a certain amount of lag. In a sense, it is concerned with yesterday's linguistics rather than today's. But it is this sophistication rather than the first kind which is probably most usable in research in language development and in reading because it has, to some extent, stood the test of time—though possibly briefly. We all know that five years is a long time in linguistics; certainly the "half life" of a linguistic idea is generally no longer than five years!

We should note, however, that this kind of linguistics is still considerably powerful. It does not deal merely with new labels for old bottles or new formalisms for old processes. It deals with new concepts and new understandings. This point cannot be overemphasized. You will understand its importance if you can appreciate the significance of the following observations. There were fundamental differences between Bloomfield (1933) and Sapir (1921). There are fundamental differences between

Chomsky (1957, 1965, 1972) and such post-Chomskyans as Postal (1971), Ross (1967), McCawley (1968), and the Lakoffs (G. Lakoff, 1970; R. Lakoff, 1968) on the one hand and Fillmore (1968) and Chafe (1970) on the other. And Labov's linguistics (1972a, 1972b) is very different again. Unless you clearly understand what is different among these linguists as well as what is the same in their views, you probably should not try to apply what they are saying to research in language development and reading. A potential researcher might evaluate his ability to do what I have just said and thereby determine his competency to do research that employs linguistic concepts.

Linguists also tend to be specialists. They categorize and sub-categorize not just into phonology, syntax, and semantics, but into sub-categories of each of these, for example, into generative phonology, and even into sub-subcategories. The result is numerous subspecialties. It may be extremely difficult to dig out from a subspecialty what might be of interest in investigations into phonic abilities or sentence processing, but such digging is probably necessary for some researchers at one time or another. In recent years investigators faced with such difficulties have occasionally tried to find refuge in such interdisciplinary havens as psycholinguistics and sociolinguistics. A warning is in order about such "avoidance" behavior. If linguistics is a branch of cognitive psychology (Chomsky's famous—or notorious—assertion) and if Labov's sociolinguistics is really the only methodologically justifiable linguistics (Labov's proselytizing claim), then psycholinguistics and sociolinguistics may turn out to be traps for the unwary, not havens for the tired. Work passed off as psycholinguistic or sociolinguistic in nature may be little more than work which had failed to confront real issues of lasting importance.

Linguistics is powerful medicine. It should be taken in small doses to avoid the risk of poisoning. But in that respect, it is neither better nor worse than statistics. Too many studies are spoiled by over-doses of statistics, as fragile or dubious linguistic concepts are subjected to massive statistical overkill. Just as it is necessary to caution against the occasional use of over-powerful ideas from linguistics in our research, so I must warn against the all too regular use of over-powerful statistical procedures employed in order to research trivia to death. Just because you can count something does not mean you have to count. And just because something is language, you do not have to treat it as though it existed in some kind of splendid isolation from everything else.

A few simple examples can be used to demonstrate the potency of linguistic medicine. In my classes I occasionally ask in a somewhat rhetorical fashion what linguistics is all about and answer by saying that its goal is the achievement of some understanding of what sounds, syllables, words, and sentences are, and how languages differ, change, and vary and yet are much the same. Students in linguistics take numerous courses designed to make them think productively about such matters. Nowhere is there a completely definitive statement covering a single one of the terms just used and nowhere is there such a statement on the subject of language change, variation, or sameness. However, you do not get quite this kind of impression from looking at books on the language arts and reading in which statements claiming to be definitive *do* abound. Of course, it is necessary to do research in the language arts and reading even though we lack a complete understanding of the basic units and processes of language. But such research should acknowledge the uncertainties that exist and should employ the most complete knowledge that is available. Unfortunately, too many researchers still confuse statements about sounds and letters; use dictionary syllabication rules as though they also characterized spoken syllabication habits; rely on sentence-parsing formulas that are patently inadequate, unrevealing, and even misleading; and are quite unclear about what is meant by such concepts as language, dialect, and rule. What we must seek therefore in research in the language arts and reading is some consideration that the researcher is linguistically alert. A few years ago there was a series of articles in *The Reading Teacher* on phonic generalizations (Burmeister, 1968; Clymer, 1963; Emans, 1967). These articles questioned a whole lot of assumptions, but not the language assumptions. Without this questioning, what was the point? It was like inspecting a building thoroughly in every other respect but deliberately ignoring the foundations!

Lest it seem that I am overselling the need for linguistics in our research, let me offer a further caution or two about linguistics as a discipline. Not only is linguistics a theoretically oriented discipline, it is also a rapidly changing one. Such change is apparently typical of a young and vital discipline. It arises from different competing ideas about what linguists should be doing, that is, about the questions they should be asking. There is no single party line one has to follow in linguistics. One result has been a profusion of polemical statements, and outsiders may be excused to some extent for using the existence of such polemics for not getting involved. After all, if linguists cannot agree among themselves on what they should be doing and on what the facts are, why should outsiders listen to linguists at all? Why not say, "A plague on all your houses!" While such rejection is understandable, it may be short-sighted. We should remember that those understandings that unite linguists far outnumber those that divide them. You do not get much progress—and intellectual excitement—out of agreeing to agree all the time. In fact, you do not get anywhere worth going. It would be unwise to ignore the linguistic consensus on such matters as the primacy of speech, the duality design-feature of language, the systematic constituent-based nature of syntax, the concept of significant contrast, and so on. These agreements exist among all the brouhaha that gets attention in some of the semipopular accounts of linguistics.

Linguistics, however, is not our only source of knowledge about language. Anthropologists, philosophers, and psychologists, for example, have all found interesting things to say about language, about the relationship of language to patterns of social organization, about the nature of linguistic acts (saying something is doing something), and about some of the mental processes that seem to be important in language use: remembering and forgetting, perceiving and processing, and thinking and imagining. Today, linguists are also beginning to take an interest in the functional uses as well as the formal properties of language. For a long time the only interest that most linguists had was in linguistic form. Now many are also interested in language function. Linguistics has become less self-centered and autonomous and more aware of other disciplines and broader issues. The previously mentioned developments of psycholinguistics and sociolinguistics are best understood as indicators of a broadening of the interests of linguists. Today, language is being studied "in context," that is, in the context of real language use. Conversations are being analyzed, linguistic variation is being acknowledged, and the purpose of speech acts is being given some of the same attention that has previously been reserved almost exclusively for the forms of speech. The problems inherent in such study are legion, and little substance has so far emerged from current concerns with what Labov has called "secular linguistics" as opposed to "closet" (or theoretical) linguistics. But at last language is regarded as dynamic and functional (that is, as something living) rather than as static and formal (that is, as something dead, fit only for a kind of ritualistic autopsy).

It would be desirable to see some of these same concerns with language as living things carried over into our research in reading. The functions of language have long interested researchers in the classroom. What has been lacking have been the necessary tools for doing good research. Perhaps the current trend in linguistics will be useful in helping us find suitable tools. But let us beware: since those tools are likely to be powerful ones, they will need to be handled with extreme caution.

Linguistics and research in reading

What are some specific suggestions and caveats regarding the use of linguistics in research in reading? Let me make some brief remarks about certain consequences of what I have just said for studies of oral language and reading, and for research in general.

Much is known about the development of language in children. There is a long history of good work and a number of exciting theoretical possibilities exist to account for the course of development, in particular in the work of McNeill (1970), Bloom (1970), Slobin (1971), Vygotsky (1962), and Piaget (1955). Nor can Skinner's work (1957) be dismissed as cavalierly as some linguists have done. A fascinating wealth of issues awaits investigation. But the days of counting are over. Hypotheses are needed which can be properly tested. Many of these should concern the various factors which impinge on language learning—mainly psychological and cultural factors heretofore largely neglected by linguists. There are lots of different linguistic ideas around; now is the time to test them against other ideas and a wide variety of data drawn from real language use. Language is a product of nature *and* nurture. We must consider *all* the variables if we are to provide a coherent account of language development, not just the one or two that our theoretical orientation requires us to see as the critical ones. The tendency to do just that is both a strength and a weakness in linguistics—a kind of powerful narrowmindedness or preoccupation results.

One particularly interesting problem has to do with how children grow up to be linguistically different from each other. We must acknowledge that linguists have long been interested in how people are the same, not how they are different—linguists swept variation under the rug rather consistently. Compare this emphasis, if you will, with the usual psychological emphasis on differences, normal distributions, and ranges of variation. Much research in linguistics glosses over differences and employs large cover terms to group subjects together. One of the most interesting developments in recent studies of child language development has been a return to intensive study of individual children, as in Brown's work (1973), for example. Children studied in this way turn out to show different developmental patterns and to use language differently. Perhaps this is one area that could be explored immediately, for such exploration could have rather interesting educational consequences.

So far as research in reading is concerned, one of the greatest needs is to look at some of the basic linguistic units employed in reading instruction—sounds, syllables, words, and sentences. What they are and how they work in the spoken language is important as are their written correlates and the nature of the correlations. Sounds and spellings, syllables and syllabication systems, words and meanings, sentences and sense—what a vast array of issues they conjure up! And what complexity! It is very easy to think of topics to research. What are the units and processes of speech perception? How do these correlate with visual units and processes? What does the eye see? How does it see? How is meaning conveyed? How linear? How predictable? How context dependent? Is it conveyed the same in writing as it is in speaking? Writing is not just simply speech put down on paper as anyone who has ever written anything knows. Moreover, the purposes of writing—and consequently of reading—are very different from those of speaking and listening, as Vygotsky (1962) observed. What is the function of reading? It is a very different function from speaking—more abstract, remote, sophisticated, specialized, and dispensable.

Of course, language is only one component in reading instruction. The linguistic system is only one system among many; systems of attention, perception, memory, and processing are also important. Language itself relies on these systems. Reading is also only one kind of information-gathering system available to people and must be seen in relation to other systems. After all, in answer to the above question about the function of reading, it may be that for many people reading is a largely unnecessary communication system.

A lot of work of high quality can be done in reading research right now because the concepts necessary for that work presently exist. But the complexity of the problems is such that healthy caution—even skepticism—is advisable. The whole area of phonics instruction needs a thorough reworking. The linguist's notion of linguistic rule is much more interesting than the reading researcher's notion of phonic generalization. The discoveries of recent years about English phonology and the hypotheses about the units and processes of phonology and the relationship of speech to writing could all bear serious examination. Children know the sound system of their language. We know something about that knowledge and we know something about orthographic principles. We need to investigate how we can use the child's knowledge of phonology on his behalf and how we can demonstrate to him what connections there are between the sounds he speaks and the letters he sees.

Studies of syntactic development and of readability can profit from the large quantities of work done on English syntax and semantics in recent years. This work has allowed us to gain many insights into just what adds to the complexity of English sentences. It is not length alone that brings about complexity. Length merely reflects complexity in a gross but not inaccurate way. Sentences are complex because of the embeddedness of clauses within them, because of quantifiers (words like *some, all, any, only*) and negatives, because of their presuppositions, entailments, and contexts, and so on. Counting this and correlating that are not enough—they represent quite trivial kinds of research activity. Counting and correlating with a computer serves only to glorify triviality.

Dialect differences continue to provide another source of research inspiration. Unfortunately *dialect* has been a much bandied about term. Individual language variation is probably just as important as those few things which unite a few speakers to constitute a "dialect" group. Much of the research presently done on dialects and reading is really research on sociocultural differences and on learning styles. The language component in such research has been simplified and attenuated to such an extent that many of the results of such research should be labeled "unsafe for any consumer." I would particularly warn about all the controversy that has swirled back and forth on the subject of "Black English," racial differences in intelligence, the "equality" of all dialects, language difference and deficiency, and so on. The literature on these topics is full of bigoted attacks on bigotry, intolerant outbursts in defense of tolerance, and passion and propaganda parading as scholarship.

A serious concern for linguistic issues could open up research in reading in ways almost undreamed of until a few years ago. Whatever reading is, it is surely a language process. Linguistics is the serious study of language. If we are ever to gain a clear understanding of reading, we must interest ourselves in the language component in reading. Linguistics is certainly our best bet if we are truly serious in increasing that understanding—and increased understanding is what research itself is all about.

REFERENCES

BLOOM, L. *Language development: form and function in emerging grammars.* Cambridge, Massachusetts: M.I.T. Press, 1970.

BLOOMFIELD, L. *Language.* New York: Holt, 1933.

BROWN, R. *A first language.* Cambridge, Massachusetts: Harvard University Press, 1973.

BURMEISTER, L. E. Usefulness of phonic generalizations. *Reading Teacher,* 1968, *21,* 349-356, 360.

CHAFE, W. L. *Meaning and the structure of language.* Chicago: University of Chicago Press, 1970.

CHOMSKY, N. *Syntactic structures.* The Hague: Mouton, 1957.

CHOMSKY, N. *Aspects of the theory of syntax.* Cambridge, Massachusetts: M.I.T. Press, 1965.

CHOMSKY, N. *Language and mind.* New York: Harcourt, Brace, Jovanovich, 1972.

CLYMER, T. The utility of phonic generalizations in the primary grades. *Reading Teacher,* 1963, *16,* 252-258.

EMANS, R. The usefulness of phonic generalizations above the primary grades. *Reading Teacher,* 1967, *20,* 419-425.

FILLMORE, C. J. The case for case. In E. Bach and R. Harms (Eds.) *Universals in linguistic theory.* New York: Holt, Rinehart and Winston, 1968.

LABOV, W. *Language in the inner city.* Philadelphia: University of Pennsylvania Press, 1972a.

LABOV, W. *Sociolinguistic patterns.* Philadelphia: University of Pennsylvania Press, 1972b.

LAKOFF, G. *Irregularity in syntax.* New York: Holt, Rinehart and Winston, 1970.

LAKOFF, R. *Abstract-syntax and Latin complementation.* Cambridge, Massachusetts: M.I.T. Press, 1968.

MC CRAWLEY, J. The role of semantics in a grammar. In E. Bach and R. Harms (Eds.) *Universals in linguistic theory.* New York: Holt, Rinehart, and Winston, 1968.

MC NEILL, D. *The acquisition of language.* New York: Harper & Row, 1970.

PIAGET, J. *The language and thought of the child.* New York: Meridian, 1955.

POSTAL, P. *Crossover phenomena.* New York: Holt, Rinehart, and Winston, 1971.

ROSS, J. R. Constraints on variables in syntax. Unpublished doctoral dissertation, M.I.T., 1967.

SAPIR, E. *Language.* New York: Harcourt, Brace and World, 1921.

SKINNER, B. F. *Verbal behavior.* New York: Appleton-Century-Crofts, 1957.

SLOBIN, D. *Psycholinguistics.* Glenview, Illinois: Scott, Foresman and Company, 1971.

VYGOTSKY, L. *Thought and language.* Cambridge, Massachusetts: M.I.T. Press, 1962.

Linguistically sound research in reading

KENNETH S. GOODMAN
University of Arizona

A psycholinguistic vantage point

Research in reading in the final quarter of the twentieth century has entered an age of science. A psycholinguistic vantage point has emerged based on a number of key premises.

These premises are simple, some will say self evident, yet they radically reorient and refocus research in reading.

Reading is now viewed as one of four language processes. Speaking and writing are productive, expressive processes. Reading, like listening, is a receptive process, no less active than writing, although the psycholinguistic activity is internal and not observable.

Readers, like listeners, speakers and writers are users of language. Communication of meaning is what language is used for. In productive language processes, speaking and writing, language is encoded; language users go from language to meaning. In receptive language processes, listening and reading, meaning is decoded; language users get meaning from language.

The new scientific premises require researchers also to see language in its social context. Language is both personal and social; it is the medium of communication and the main vehicle of human thought and learning.

Written language development in human societies comes after oral language development, at the point where communication must extend over time and space.

For individuals, written language almost always also comes after oral language development. It comes at the point where the individual in a literate society recognizes the personal need for moving beyond face-to-face communication to interact with unseen, perhaps unknown writers.

So far nothing I've said is either the result of research or profound theoretical insights. These premises represent a point of view in the most literal sense of that phrase. One need only look at reading to see them. They are in no need of scientific verification since they are so evident— that is, provided that one looks directly at reading.

Conventional wisdom

Unfortunately many people, including researchers, have not begun consideration of reading from the simple direct vantage point that would lead to awareness of these premises. The study of language in general, in fact, has been plagued by the tendency to proceed from unexamined traditional beliefs about language. Conventional wisdom about language is so deeply rooted that even researchers committed to scientific method and logic often plunge into research on language and language learning with no attempt at consideration of the facts of linguistic reality.

The known and the unknowable

Many research studies are further hampered by use of one of two opposite but widely accepted views: In the first view, language is treated as being so well understood that it does not need examination. This translates to such statements as, "Everybody knows that _____." This view in reading is one of the reasons the public is always so susceptible to attacks on current reading instruction. Since everybody knows that the way to teach reading is through phonics, it follows that programs that aren't phonics programs must be the work of idiots or a deliberate conspiracy to keep kids from learning to read.

On the other hand it is very popular for people speaking on reading to take the opposite view: Language is an unfathomable mystery. It is unknowable. This leads to justification of personal ignorance, by statements like, "Nobody knows how reading works, therefore . . ." This then becomes a rationale for trial and error—particularly in methods and materials. If no one knows how reading works, anything is worth trying.

An obligation to be scientific

But language processes—reading included—are neither universally understood nor unknowable. This leads me to my final premise: Those conducting research in reading have an obligation to begin on a base of scientific insight and understanding. They must move to a clear unobstructed vantage point in looking at language, and they must become familiar with the best available theory and knowledge. Furthermore, they must use tools appropriate to psycholinguistic research.

Linguistic insights from theory and research

Research and scholarly thought have provided a number of insights about reading which expand on the base of the premises I've outlined. Both research and theory are in dynamic stages. That means that new knowledge is being produced at a rapid rate. It also means that there are competing theories and conflicting findings emerging. This condition is not justification for ignoring progress or reversion to a golden age when things seemed simpler. It is just such a dynamic state of affairs that opens up whole new directions in research—provided the research community can hang loose and remain open to innovation.

Some highly productive insights from scientific language study have emerged in the past decade and a half:

1. All children develop language competence. This development is so universal and rapid that some scholars have concluded that language is essentially not learned but innate. What is most remarkable is that children acquire not just a set of rules for generating new language; they can say things they've never heard.

2. Language acquisition relates to human need for communication. The mechanisms and motivation for acquisition of language operate in both written and oral language.

3. Language difference is to be expected. Language grows and changes to meet the changing needs of its users. Difference must never be confused with deficiency. Your dialect is not a funny way of speaking mine.

4. Language is learned in the context of its communicative use. Learners treat it like concrete learning if it is meaningful, and the meaning is relevant and significant to them. Language is only abstract when it is fragmented and/or divorced from meaningful use.

5. Language competence and language behavior are not the same. Competence results in behavior; it is the control over the process which results in behavior. Behavior reflects but is not equivalent to performance.

6. To infer the competence from behavioral indicators, it's useful to postulate a deep language structure and set of rules for generating the observable surface phenomena.

7. Research in reading must be process oriented, it must use behavioral indicators to infer underlying competence.

8. The human brain is the organ of information processing. As such, it directs the eye and ear and makes selective use of its input channels. Perception in reading is largely a matter of what we expect to see. In oral reading the mouth says what the brain directs it to say, not what the eye sees.

9. Effective reading is achieving coherent meaning. Efficient reading gets to meaning with the least amount of effort necessary, and uses minimal perceptual input.

10. Language processes, reading included, cannot be usefully studied by reducing them to manipulation of constituent units such as letters or words or distorting them by looking at them in highly limited and unusual circumstances.

11. Reading, like all language processes, must be studied in the personal and social contexts which give it purpose.

Even if researchers find it hard to accept some of these things I've labeled productive insights, they should still be generating exciting research if only in the attempt to reject them or demonstrate an alternative explanation of the phenomena involved.

Popular unenlightened and unenlightening research practice

I've suggested earlier some key reasons why reading researchers have not begun with an awareness of linguistic realtiy. I'd like to explore now some reasons intrinsic to popular research practice that might explain why so much research in reading is both unenlightened and unenlightening.

Narrow vision

Researchers frequently operate within very narrow frameworks. They often pluck a small item out of current practice or select a question of concern only within a specific program of reading instruction as the basis for their research. An example might be to study an experimental method of "teaching consonant blends." Such research not only suffers from being of value only within the narrow methodological context in which such instruction is used but it also suffers from the usual failure to examine the relationship of the item selected to the general question of children learning to read.

Restrictive models

Research on reading instruction has tended to be dominated by research design models which are of limited value in providing useful information on teaching and learning. This seems to stem from a desire to achieve "rigor" and respectability without a sound theoretical base. Most common is the use of the *experimental-control group design*. An attempt is made to obtain significance, reliability, and validity through careful manipulation of data using statistics based on mathematical probability theory.

Some pitfalls in the use of *experimental methodology* are fairly well known:

- Variables are hard to control. Too much is happening in classrooms that can't be monitored and regulated.
- Control "treatments" are usually poorly described and poorly controlled.
- Unwarranted assumptions are made that all experimental classrooms are equal and interchangeable as are all control classrooms.
- It isn't possible to control learning which takes place outside of school, planned and unplanned.
- Results of instruction may not show in any measurable sense until long after it is received. "Results" of short term experimental studies are therefore unreliable.
- Some important aspects of reading are unassessable in any quantifiable sense.
- Conclusions are usually based on performance on norm or criterion referenced tests. Such performance may not adequately represent gains in competence.

But there are more basic reasons for rejecting the experimental model as a basic tool in research on reading and reading instruction.

At best it can only "prove" or "disprove" a small set of hypotheses already believed to be true. It plows no new ground, provides no new insights.

The requirement for mass data and random samples causes a focus only on central tendencies in statistics, whereas individual variation and deviation may be most enlightening. We count "right" answers instead of examining wrong ones.

Manipulation of data—however rigorously it's conducted—can never make up for the original poor quality of the data itself. Sound data can only come from a base of knowledge, sound assumptions, and a theoretical framework that give the data value.

Of what value is it to prove everyone does something if understanding *how* one person does it is what we really need to know?

Data worshipping

Sometimes it seems that research itself becomes confused with data collection and manipulation. There are so many elegant processes available, particularly with easy access to packaged computer statistical programs, that correlate, regress, factor analyze, and otherwise cause data to engage in impressive behavior, that meaningful results are lost.

Having produced tables, charts, arrays, and matrices, researchers engage in *ex post datum* speculation about why the statistical relationships exist, what to do about achieving them if they are good, or which should be eliminated because they are bad. Judgment as to whether they are good or bad is often made on a common sense level.

In reading and reading instruction with multitudes of texts, tests, workbooks, readability formulas, and management systems available, it's easy to generate great quantities of data. Making sense of the data, before or after statistical manipulation, requires some knowledge of what reading is and how it is learned.

Reifying tests

Tests are always developed to provide insights into phenomena not readily obtainable in the course of ongoing observation, teaching, or learning. A test maker builds a test which he hopes will reveal, through test performance, the competence he is seeking to examine. Building a valid test requires much more than administering it to various standard-izaion groups to establish statistical norms as well as statistical reliability and validity. Building a test requires a theoretical model of the competence to be examined, based on adequate research and knowledge. Sub-tests, items, and tasks must relate to reality through this model. This requirement is as true for criterion referenced as for norm referenced tests.

When a researcher constructs his own test he is generally held responsible for demonstrating the validity both through theoretical and statistical means. But if he uses someone else's test—particularly one published and in wide use—he is absolved of such responsibility.

Researchers frequently equate performance on a test in reading with reading itself. Each subtest—"vocabulary," "paragraph meaning," "word recognition"—is assumed to be a real isolatable competence or aspect of a general competence called *reading*, and research data are reported not as test performance but as if the competence itself were being measured. Researchers rarely say "The subjects had poor performance on the subtest on paragraph comprehension." They simply say the subjects had poor paragraph comprehension. The reading test becomes reality itself, and the researcher often does not go beyond test performance in considering the significance of data. Too often in research reports *reading is performance on reading tests*.

Confusing science and technology

A contemporary madness results from the assumptions that all uses of mechanization, industrial organization, cybernetics, and other aspects of technology are scientific. Technology is treated as a synonym for science. It's as if people think that all that was necessary to get humans on the moon was to build a rocketship to get them there. Humanity couldn't have gotten there, as far as present science knows, without one; but science made both the trip and the needed technology possible.

Linguistically sound research

Furthermore, there are infinite numbers of uses of space technology that are possible which are worthless, absurd, or both.

In reading instruction and reading research, worthless and/or absurd uses of technology are frequently treated as scientific. Computer assisted instruction, computerized data gathering, instructional management systems are being built on wholly unscientific assumptions and views. They produce neat, manipulable data which are treated with unwarranted respect by researchers, who are awed by their technological trappings.

Technology can be, in fact must be, used to facilitate learning; but educational researchers are scientists who must control their tools and not become controlled by them. Nor can they retreat from their obligation to people into the impersonal comfort of the machine, the data, or the management system.

Recreating the world in the laboratory image

Researchers often create simplified versions of phenomena and experimental designs in their laboratories in order to study the world or some aspect of it which is too complex for direct study. Under special experimental conditions they can gain useful insights. The goal is then to test these insights against reality. But in reading and language research particularly, there has been a strong tendency to view reality as an extension of the laboratory and the narrow experimental view. Phenomena isolated for study are treated as unchanged from their occurrence in uncontrolled reality. This is a problem of great concern when researchers or others leap from research to development of reading methods and materials. There is a real world, and ideas—however cleverly tested in the narrow confines of the laboratory—must also be placed in the context of this real world.

Mindless empiricism

Objectivity in reading research is often construed to mean that only the tangible, measurable, directly observable aspects of things are legitimate concerns. Values, philosophical positions, theories are viewed as unnecessary, subjective, and dangerous.

What often results is a mindless empiricism of the sort demonstrated by the Blind Men of Hindustan. "All we know is what we can measure" seems to be the motto of these researchers. They are content to stay on the surface of things, to add, but not to synthesize. They particularly reject consideration of values. In the name of scientific objectivity they disdain responsibility for the effects of their studies. No field of knowledge has been able to progress without theory to explain observational phenomena, to generate hypotheses, to predict behavior. Reading knowledge has tended not to move or build on research because of rigorously superficial, atheoretical research which has prevailed.

Atheoretical research often produces absurd conclusions which are apparently supported by empirical studies and are accepted even though they contradict the reality practitioners must deal with. Recent testing in California, for example, appeared to show that disproportionate numbers of Chicano and black school age children suffered from aphasia as compared to other populations. One must regard this conclusion as unlikely if not absurd, if these data are placed in the context of what is known about language development and language and cultural difference. In that context, we would do better to reconsider the tests than to group children and build curricula based on the results.

The dissertation process

Doctoral research ought to provide opportunities for scholars to explore the frontiers of reading. Yet one of the most conservative influences on reading research is the dissertation process. The doctoral candidate often is up-to-date in his or her knowledge of research and thought. The student should select a current problem or issue and utilize innovative research methodology. He or she ought to know more about the topic and methodology than the chairman or the members of the committee of three to five faculty members, each of whom may view reading research from a somewhat outdated vantage point. By the time he or she has satisfied a committee and an archaic set of university requirements, the researcher may have been forced to compromise methodology, to touch irrelevant bases, to answer already answered questions. If he or she has built a background in linguistics and psycholinguistics, committee members may defend their ignorance by belittling the significance of the knowledge, insights, or vantage point being used. Often the effect is to push a student back to safe studies with traditional instruments. Sometimes the student perseveres, but the study is cluttered and weakened by conditions imposed by committee members. Universities and doctoral committees must give serious thought to opening up the dissertation process and liberating students from the yoke of tradition.

The funding process

Similarly, the process by which research gets funded works in a conservative manner. Proposals are read and judged by those who have made their mark and have vested interests in the status quo. Traditions of what "good" research proposals look like grow up which make it difficult to tell the ingenious innovator from the crack pot. Official requests for proposals often are written in a language and conceptual framework which eliminates alternate, productive models.

Furthermore researchers must "go where the money is" rather than deal with research that needs to be done and which they are competent to do. Sometimes research support goes to those who can include the right timely key words in their proposals.

Another problem is that money goes to money. New researchers with great ideas but no past funding find it hard to get that first grant. Universities and funding agencies both need to expand their support of high-risk research.

The research pecking order

Researchers like other human beings tend to be influenced in their attitudes toward others—by their perception of the status of those others relative to their own status. So psychologists are in awe of some linguists but show disdain for educational researchers and their work. This status-conscious view causes some researchers from disciplines other than education to be less careful in doing their homework when beginning research in reading. Sometimes they don't bother to find out what's already known. Sometimes they are unscholarly in the way they loosely interpret their data. Sometimes they state opinions authoritatively which have no basis in their research, particularly when extrapolating from data to methodological applications. Conversely, eductional researchers sometimes show the up-tight, self-conscious behavior of the low-status group member who accepts the derogatory stereotype of his group. They become ever more conservative and narrow in theory, methodology, and research scope than the "pure" scientists they emulate. Practical, applied research enjoys less status in many disciplines than pure research which pursues knowledge for its own sake.

Research oriented to the solution of real problems—illiteracy for example—is treated as unworthy. That view is reflected in promotion, salary, and research support policies of universities. It influences acceptance policies of research journals. It has even had effects on federally funded programs designed to deal with real problems.

It is becoming increasingly clear that sound research in reading is going to require an interdisciplinary base. But interdisciplinary teams will achieve their goals only if they can operate in a climate of mutual respect. Elitism in any form has no place in research planning, funding, or performance.

Broad jumps and other leaps

Reading has been particularly plagued by a tendency for "methods" of instruction and sets of materials for instruction to be built by researchers or consumers of research on the basis of single conclusions from narrow or limited research. Researchers have the obligation to be cautious in generalizing from research conclusions to implications for practice. They also need to be careful when they change hats and become authors of basal reading texts that they consider all necessary inputs, become informed about all relevant concerns, and operate with the same scientific cautions which they employ in their research.

Early uses of linguistic concepts in reading research led to the so-called "linguistic method" and a rash of "linguistic readers," all based on a single linguistic principle of minimal differences between phonemes. Phonics programs were renamed "decoding" programs to capitalize on a popular misconception that learning to read was "decoding" phonemes to graphemes. Better instruction will result from scientifically based research but not in a simple direct way. Research is needed on how reading works, how it is learned, how effective various programs for instruction are. The knowledge from such research must then be integrated with other practical knowledge to produce more effective instruction and more universal learning.

What are the requirements of good reading research?

Some of the reasons for poor or nonproductive research have been explored above. In contrast, here are some of the requirements for linguistically sound reading research. Simply speaking, the more that's known about reading, the more necessary it is for researchers to base their studies on a wide understanding of what is known. Research must be consistent with modern insight into language and language learning.

Research studies of large numbers of subjects must give way to depth studies of small numbers, such as those popular in linguistics and developmental psycholinguistics. If a researcher can find through the study of a single subject how reading is used to comprehend a writer's message, an important contribution will be made to human knowledge.

Real people using real language in various real situations must be the objects of research if we are to understand reading as it really is. Research problems are being generated today from a variety of productive sources.

Theories and models

As we attempt to understand the phenomena observable in reading acquisition, models and theories are emerging. These models produce predictions and hypothetical explanations of reading phenomena. Very useful studies can emerge designed to support or reject these theories, models, and hypotheses. Studies which provide data which are consistent or inconsistent with a theoretical view will make clear whether any existing

Linguistically sound research

model is most useful in dealing with reading. The models become more powerful as they are tested against reality and our knowledge of the reading process grows at the same time.

Anomolies

Another base for generating useful research in reading is in the numerous unexplained anomolies which now exist. For example:

- Why do virtually all children acquire oral language without professional assistance yet some children don't seem to learn to read easily and well?
- Why do schools appear to be less successful in teaching reading to boys than girls, blacks than whites, poor kids than rich ones? Too often we start from the "fact" of the difference in achievement and speculate on cause. We need to understand why and in what ways we're less successful with some groups of kids than others.
- Why, in a literate society with universal access to instruction, do some people remain functionally illiterate?

Rejected absurdity

As we come to understand more about the reading process, much useful research can come from reexamining the absurd findings of less enlightened research. Why do some groups have low norms on IQ and achievement tests? (We know it isn't a real difference.) Why has knowledge of the alphabet been a fair predictor of later performance on reading tests? Why do even ridiculous instructional programs succeed in helping some kids to learn to read?

Unsolved real problems

Bold new approaches to real problems in building the knowledge base necessary to achieve universal literacy are possible and necessary as the reality comes into focus.

A key example of an urgent unsolved problem is how to get at the competence underlying reading comprehension. In this, as in many other questions, it's easier to see what's wrong with current solutions and practice than to develop new approaches. We know that all current techniques try to infer comprehension competence from post reading performance. Such inference is never really adequate. It is always distorted.

Another major unsolved question is how much the silent reading process differs from the much more easily studied oral reading process.

These questions frustrate but they also tantalize. Probably breakthroughs will come from interdisciplinary teams, drawing on knowledge and methodology from linguistics, psychology, and education.

The time has come

    It is not unreasonable to ask *now* that researchers bring a modern base of knowledge to their research. It is not unreasonable to expect them to conduct research worthy of time, effort, and expense—research which, whether big or small, contributes to some degree to movement toward the goal of universal literacy.

Social aspects of working with the schools

NICHOLAS J. ANASTASIOW
Indiana University

In addition to the more technical design and measurement problems of reading research, there are more practical aspects involved in the management of entering into, operating within, and exiting from school situations in which one conducts research. This article will give examples of the "social" problems of school research and provide specific statements, regarding generalizations that have been derived from experience, to aid in conducting research in school settings. The comments are meant to apply to both small scale (one class) and large scale (many class) research projects.

Entering the school

The researcher should recognize that educational research is not highly valued by the schools; in fact, it often is perceived as unimportant. In my opinion, school personnel far too often seem more interested in proving that something they don't like is "bad" than they are in gathering data to support their practices. In the past, many studies which have used children in school settings have been highly criticized, and often justifiably. The major criticism school people have made of the educational researcher is that the research isn't practical and hasn't helped the school, teacher, or student. More important, the teacher frequently suspects that "pure" research doesn't add to "science" as researchers claim, nor add to the basic fund of knowledge. Therefore, before the researcher contacts the schools, some attention must be given to the question of why a school would want him to do the research in their setting. He should be convinced that what he wants to do is worth the time teachers and children will devote to his task. In addition, he should have developed a rationale that he can explain and defend to the school personnel. Once the research worker has developed a rationale, he should be cautious as to what he promises the school. Frequently, in our desire to secure a school population, we promise too much. I refer to this as the "Panacea Trap." Educators have tended to see each new innovation as a panacea for solving all their problems. Research workers sometimes have become over-enthusiastic as to what their research will demonstrate if their hypotheses are supported.

My best advice on how to initiate entrance into a school is to call the central office of the school to find out if there are specific sets of procedures for gaining permission to conduct research in their schools. Once these procedures have been identified, follow them in every respect. If it is not included, add to whatever procedures the school may have personal contact with each member in the hierarchy related to your research. For example, if the superintendent approves the project, be sure to contact the principal of the school directly and in person. Inexperienced researchers frequently will by-pass the principal and contact teachers directly. This is so serious a mistake that I would suspect few researchers with any experience in conducting research in schools will do so without first securing the full cooperation of the principal. The principal sets the tone of the building and can do much to facilitate or, more importantly, subvert your efforts.

I also am of the opinion that the principal has the right to know the full details of the research, and it is the obligation of the researcher to fully inform the principal and answer any questions he might have. The stimulation you may provide him by discussing your ideas with him may be the ultimate service you perform for the school. The principal's role is often one of isolation, and he tends to enjoy discussing ideas with outside personnel.

Following attainment of the principal's approval, ask for and gently insist upon a meeting with the teachers, preferably after school or at their lunch period. Frequently, a principal will want to take you directly to a classroom at the time you are to do your research, and you will find that he has not asked the teacher's permission to participate in the project. I would hesitate to conduct research with children from classes where the teacher has not been allowed to examine the instruments to be administered and ask questions as to the purpose of the research. Many schools will require that you inform parents that their child is to take part in a research project. A letter informing parents of the project containing a brief description of the goals and objectives of the research is usually all that is necessary. The phrase, "If you have any questions regarding the project, please call _____" is usually sufficient to secure the cooperation of most parents.

Increasingly, teacher associations and unions are playing a decision making role in school districts. Be sure to check with the superintendent's office for guidelines as to the union's role in the school district where you plan to conduct research. There may be limitations as to when you can meet with teachers and the teacher's role in participating with the research project. A check with the union representative will help clarify the local policy.

A productive researcher on the west coast has very little problem obtaining large research populations—usually as often as he desires. The generalizations I have stated above are drawn from his behavior. He always meets the principal in an unhurried manner and later meets with the teacher or teachers to be involved. If asked, he reports his general findings to the parent group or speaks on any other topic of the PTA's choice that is within his realm of competence. For one research project, he was able to secure without a single objection from principal, teacher, or parents, the entire fourth grade population, which was located in 22 schools.

Political pressure groups and pet theories

If you are planning on trying out a departure from the school's regular program—for example a linguistic program in contrast to a phonics program—take care to explore fully with the superintendent or his representative whether or not you will encounter emotional resistances due to pet theories in the district. Occasionally, a research worker will unknowingly find himself the center of a district-wide political campaign due to the fact that his research appears to counter a prejudice on the part of a minority of the school population. For example, recently the director of a national study had to fly to a school on the west coast and appear before an open schoolboard meeting because one of the stories in his material, which dealt with population data, was misinterpreted as family life education by one of the schoolboard members. Studies that deal with reading comprehension may contain innocent paragraphs of content that are unacceptable to some local groups. In addition, there usually are other research projects being conducted in the school district. If these projects have an opposing orientation to the one you plan to conduct, explore whether your project will be perceived as a threat to the conductors of the original project.

In one study in which I was involved, a schoolboard member was the coauthor with the reading supervisor of an experimental reading series. He was extremely hostile toward evaluation of his project and, more important, perceived all other research projects in reading as rivals.

School district personnel frequently will reject your project as a protective device to avoid any and all public-relations problems. Therefore, it is best to explore with them directly whether or not your project will cause conflict. The open discussion does two things: 1) it often will make it possible for you to conduct your research because it will give you the opportunity to reassure them that you will not cause a problem; and 2) if your project possesses a potential threat to some group, you will be saved the embarrassment of having your study used for political purpose by local newspapers or board members running in local elections. I have endured both experiences and enjoyed neither of them at that time nor in retrospect.

The nature of the child sample

Make an attempt to verify the nature of the social class status of the children you are to test. Walk around the neighborhood and observe for yourself the general characteristics of the school to determine whether the outward look of the homes meets your expectation. You can often be fooled by the arithmetic mean the school has available. The data may look typical, but may be a result of dichotomous groups. For example, in an upper-middleclass school, we discovered a trailer court hidden behind a high hedge. The trailer court children had just been transferred to the school. The mean achievement level of two-thirds of the class was the eightieth percentile. The remaining one-third, the trailer court children, were achieving at the fortieth percentile level. Combined, the total group mean score was in the 60s. In another study, we were led to believe we were dealing with an economically depressed population. When we entered the classroom, many children did not look like the typical deprived group. Particularly, their clothes indicated a higher purchasing power. More important, they were extremely verbal children and spoke standard vernacular. We discovered that a number of graduate students attending a medical school across the street entered their children in these classes. As you know, graduate students make very little money, so the children qualified on economic grounds for these classes.

Asking the principal whether he uses any type of special grouping procedures may uncover some unique styles. In one school, we found six sections of the sixth grade. The principal indicated to us that he had assigned to a teacher who had majored in psychology all of the more serious emotional problems. To a second class, he had assigned a former high school teacher and had given her the major behavior-control problems. The other four classes were, he reported, rather placid, which greatly reduced his work since this made it necessary for him to deal with only two teachers instead of six.

In every case it is best to secure a larger sample size than needed for your research because the problems listed above are usually uncovered after the fact. In many cases you will have to discard data. Thus, having a larger sample than needed will save your study.

Creating a positive climate

If you are to use only some classes in a school, offer to meet with the other teachers to share your expertise. You need not discuss your experiment if knowledge of the treatment will interfere with your study. Talking about new trends in research as in reading or language arts will help create a positive atmosphere for you and your associates. Although the class or children may not be ready for you when you are ready to administer your instruments, do not mistake the teacher's scheduling problem as not caring about punctuality. Nothing is as disturbing to a teacher as having a class ready and then having the researcher arrive five to ten minutes late. The same principle holds for your appointment with teachers to describe your study. Many times you will have to make the decisions about being on time by insisting that you leave the principal's office even though he appears to be very relaxed about the time. Recently, we were to explain our study to all the teachers from three schools at 1:00 p.m. The principals took us out to lunch and we were all engaged in a lively discussion about schools. When we asked how long it would take to drive to the meeting place, they said, "Not long." We grew increasingly anxious en route, as 1:00 p.m. approached and the drive was much farther than we expected. An icy silence greeted us when we arrived late, and it continued to envelop the room. We attempted to place a share of the blame on the principals by noting that their generous Southern hospitality had caused us to be late, but that only made matters worse. It was more than an hour before we felt we had the group of teachers with us.

Teachers desire all children to take the instruments and share in the rewards. It is difficult for teachers to accept the notion of a random sample. If it is feasible, administer your instrument to the whole class and select your sample from the total group. In some studies where time consuming individual testing is done, this procedure is impractical. However, if you institute a behavior modification study in which rewards are administered to only part of the class, teachers will desire you to provide the whole class with some type of reward following the study.

Space

Most schools have limited space for extra projects. If your research requires a special room for administering your instruments, you may find that you will conduct your study in unique settings. I have administered instruments in supply rooms, the teachers' lounge, basements, picnic-lunch bench areas, hallways, cafeterias, and in one case, the outer section of a bathroom. The principal who is truly willing to cooperate with your study usually will find some place for you, even though you may have to operate on a highly flexible schedule. For example, our schedule for collecting language data in one large metropolitan school was as follows: On Mondays and Wednesdays we used the speech room and, on Tuesdays and Thursdays, the auditorium. On Fridays we had a corner hall which led to a dead end. This required our research assistant to move the equipment daily and on some days, when a "surprise" program was held in the auditorium, to cancel her appointments. If you can use the total class, you have greatly simplified your procedures, but have not—as we shall see in the next section—totally solved your problem. In some cases, we have rented a small trailer. By placing the trailer close to the school building, children can be brought to the testing site easily. Of course, the principal's permission should be obtained before renting a trailer.

Administering the instruments

I would suggest that in all possible instances the teacher should not administer your research instruments. Teachers are prone to want to assist children and frequently will provide nonverbal cues to help them solve problems. On some occasions, teachers, wanting the child to meet with success, will provide direct help. And in some, hopefully rare, instances the teacher in his or her anxiety for the class to do well will actually provide children with answers. If this occurs, your only option is to destroy the data. I maintain we are guests in a teacher's classroom, and what we observe is privileged information. If a teacher intentionally helps children, we are in an ethical position of destroying the data but not the teacher. In all cases, I would recommend trained research technicians or the researcher himself administer all instruments. In this respect, it is recommended that all pilot studies be conducted by the principal investigator. Usually, only you, the principal investigator, will be able to make decisions when emergencies arise. Once all the details have been worked out, others can collect the data for you. Teachers on leave make excellent research assistants. They have the advantage of knowing the school and of being accepted by classroom teachers; they are familiar with school regulations and are confident in handling individual or groups of children. In some states, having a credentialed teacher as your research assistant reduces many school-related problems due to legal constraints on who is legally able to supervise children. Teachers on leave readily respond to training and are usually very cooperative research associates.

Occasionally, one finds himself in a classroom where the teacher feels highly threatened by the researcher. Fortunately, not too many teachers show abnormal behavior patterns, but in almost every school district there is at least one teacher whose room should be avoided. Be sure to ask the principal if there are any teachers in his school who should not take part in the study for any reason. I do not suggest you probe to find out the reason; accept the common excuse for pathology given by a principal: for example, "Teacher X has had a great many family, health and/or personal problems."

In establishing rapport with children, ask them if they know what they are going to do with you. With young children, we most frequently tell teachers to inform their class they are going to play a game. One child, while walking from the first to the fourth floor of the building, revealed that he was afraid we were going to electrocute him if he wasn't good. We pursued the issue, asking why he should think such a thing, and found that was what his teacher had informed the entire class. Due to the fact that we were using head sets and tape recorders, we had to eliminate the class from our sample. Clearly this teacher was disturbed with the children—or with us. In either case, the data obtained would not be valid.

The unexpected and interrupted

We were administering a self-concept measure to a second grade class in an economically depressed area in Tennessee. Half-way through the administration, the principal came into the room and whispered to the teacher. The teacher then came over and asked if she could speak to me. My two research assistants asked the children to wait a minute. To make matters short, a local merchant of a Mexican restaurant had arrived unannounced at the school with frito chips, Mexican hats, and a pinata filled with goodies. He insisted that he only had one-half hour. The principal said that the rest of the school was gathered around the flagpole, and he and the teacher wondered if I wanted the class I was testing to be left out of the activity in order to finish the administration of the instrument. The choice was not a research choice; it was a moral one. Did I have the right to continue the administration of a measure and keep one class of children from the excitement that was going on outside? We stopped the administration, went outside, ate frito chips, donned Mexican hats, and watched the children scramble for the candy and toys once the pinata was broken. As we came back in, my graduate assistant asked, "How valid will these tests be?" Cheered by the relevance of my student's question I said, "It's a researchable question, but after we allow the children to finish the task, we'll probably throw these tests away. If you are interested, we can design a study to measure the impact of a perceived-to-be-positive experience on children's self-reports." In other words, most large-scale, so-called research projects in the school are opportunities to identify and generate hypotheses, and should be perceived as such.

Major interruptions occur with such frequency that I almost expect a fire drill to occur while I am in a school. Last February the principal did warn me he was to have a drill that morning, so I was prepared. But I was not ready—nor was the principal—for the four fire engines, one hook and ladder truck, ambulance, and three police cars that arrived at the building. His remark to the fireman bears repeating. He said, "I'm sorry. I've only been here five years and I keep forgetting to call the station to warn you of my drill." The response by the fireman is of interest but is X rated.

What I am saying is that I, like the principal, have only been here a few years; and research in the schools is a source of continuous surprise. Classes will be on field trips, at a puppet play, in another room, or listening to a story in the library. Much more difficult to handle is the situation in which the class may have just gone through a negative experience with the teacher. A colleague of mine was administering an experimental form of a reading test in a classroom in which a piano had been pushed against the two sides of one corner to make a triangular space. While he was handing out the instrument, a small voice came from that space: "Sir, I don't have a copy." Recently we went to a rural first grade classroom to conduct a trial session of our language curriculum. We noticed that a young girl was sitting in a pool of liquid, and the teacher had not excused her nor offered her any assistance. When we asked the teacher what had happened, she said, "She always wets during music." I was rather surprised when my colleague quietly said, "Perhaps that was the most appropriate response to the lesson."

Leaving the school

After your research project has been completed, a letter should be sent to all parents whose children took part in the study. The letter should be written in lay terms summarizing the major findings and thanking parents for their cooperation. This action will do much to insure your continuing acceptance by the schools and parent community for future research projects. Occasionally a parent may wish to know more about the research, and your phone number included in the letter with an invitation to call for additional information will satisfy this need. The letters can be sent home via the schools or appear in the school's newsletter, if one exists. In one study, we were able to maintain contact with over 90 percent of our research population over a period of four years. In some cases, parents who had moved from the school district informed us of their new locations and volunteered their child's continuance in the study.

I also recommend that any journal article should footnote thanks to the school district involved. In some rare cases, where the data may reflect unfavorably upon the schools, personnel should be given the option as to whether they are identified specifically.

Reporting: the last major step in the research act

BRUCE TONE
Editorial Associate
Reading Research Quarterly

The importance of effective reporting

The most compelling, original, and carefully executed research will have minimal impact until its findings are communicated. Although research is a worthy acitivity in and of itself, its primary aim is to increase man's knowledge; and it cannot do that unless it is reported clearly. It must be logically organized, complete, and clearly and carefully written. So essential is the need to report research effectively that it is argued here that reporting is the last major step of the research act and that the impact of all the vital steps in conducting good research ultimately depends on it.

Although research is often reported verbally, more often it is written; and this chapter focuses on that method. Most of the points considered, however, are applicable to both forms of reporting. A discussion of how audience awareness can help insure a good report precedes a relatively prescriptive analysis of the essential sections a complete report should include. The chapter concludes with the consideration of some miscellaneous concerns, most of which are related to specific style problems. Much of the material in the chapter has accrued from encounters with manuscripts on reading research that had been critiqued and edited by experts in the field. Consequently, this discussion frequently clarifies what a report ought to do by pointing out what some researchers unfortunately do instead. If that treatment is reminiscent of composition courses, consider that research reporting is essentially just good exposition, the goal of all freshman composition teachers and manuals.

Audience awareness

Adopting the reader's point of view

Editorial analysis of research manuscripts reveals how closely related clear thinking is to clear reporting. That is not to imply that when the researcher reports ineffectively, he does not understand his material. Rather, intense involvement in the material sometimes betrays the researcher when it is time to write the report. The researcher is so close to the material that it is extremely difficult for him to remember the audience's uninformed condition and to recognize the need to arrange the report logically from that point of view. Also, the researcher, who is so familiar with the subjects, materials, and procedures, may gloss over or omit details the reader needs in order to understand the report. Sometimes the reader's understanding is muddled because synthesis that occurred in the researcher's mind during his activity goes unexplained in the report. These problems are avoided by adopting an awareness of one's audience.

Selecting an audience and a vehicle

The audience to be considered must be selected first, however; and that selection is the result of the thinking the researcher does in choosing a vehicle. This selection will be effected by the material itself and by the audience the writer wants to reach with that material. A publisher for the practitioner audience, for example, would be much more interested in a study with immediate classroom implications than in one with implications primarily for future research. And the practitioner audience would be more interested in those implications than in the design or implementation of the research. Thus a report written for such a journal may need to frame that relevance from the outset. An audience of fellow researchers, however, is usually suspicious of a report that begins by stressing implications; and a journal published for such an audience may require a presentation that delays dealing with the implications until the reader has a chance to examine the study and its findings.

Even within audiences, specific publications may treat reports differently. In so doing, they tend to cultivate a more specific audience, which comes to expect the kind of reporting that attracted it in the first place. Sometimes a publication's "style" of reporting is controlled by its need to marry its audience's priorities to the economic factors in publishing. Such considerations may affect the choice of subject matter as well as how extensively it can be treated.

The researcher's concern in all of this is one of awareness. After determining the appropriate audience, the researcher must target a logical publication as a vehicle for the report. The process then reverses. The nature of the vehicle selected and its particular audience act as levers on the reporter and may modify the intentions for reporting the research.

By carefully selecting a vehicle and by then preparing the report specifically for submission to that publication, a researcher considerably improves the chances of getting a report of good research published. One way to do this is to examine carefully both the kinds of reports a publication has been printing and any stated intentions of its editors to publish broader content. Many journals have manuals or guides that give authors clear indication of the kind of material the editors accept. Such guides also detail procedures for submission that, if heeded, can insure the consideration of the manuscript.

A publication's audience can be determined from information supplied by the publisher, but some simple reasoning can also prepare the researcher to write with an appropriate audience in mind. A research oriented publication, such as *The Journal of Reading Behavior* or the *Reading Research Quarterly*, will have an audience of researchers, college teachers, specialists, and graduate students from both the specific field and from numerous related fields. Though varied, such an audience has a common sophisticated interest in the field, and it is not difficult to determine at what level explanations must begin and what the audience in general expects from the report. At the same time, the diversity of such an audience underlines the need for clarity and precision so that each reader can easily identify the relevance the research reported has for her or him.

Outlining the essentials with the audience in mind

Audience awareness stresses that the organization of a research report ought to be structured from the reader's point of view. As in any good essay, the reader expects a general structure that moves from an introduction through a development to a conclusion. Within this structure, the readers of research journals expect to learn what was done, why it was done, how it was done, and what the outcome was—and preferably in that order. Thus, the careful delineation of a problem, the development of a rationale, the execution of an appropriate design, and the analysis of results can help guarantee a well organized report; for the author has full control of his material from the outset. A logical consideration of how the reader can best comprehend this material leads to meaningful organization, which in turn facilitates clear writing. A strong organization especially guarantees effective transition between parts and also between paragraphs.

In most instances where good intentions to cover all of the essentials end up in muddled reporting, the researcher would have been greatly aided by outlining the report before beginning writing. Bearing in mind the logical requirement that the exposition begin, develop, and conclude, the reporter of research can translate the journalistic requirements of what, why, and how into the more specific sections that a research report should include: a brief but direct explanation of exactly what the study did; a statement of the problem and a discussion of the background and rationale for the study; a review of related literature; any hypotheses being studied; a description of the procedures used, including a full account of the instruments used, the statistical techniques employed, the population studied, and any steps used in collecting the data; a discussion of the limitations and assumptions of the study; a presentation of the findings; interpretations of the findings; conclusions drawn on the findings; and a discussion of the implications of the findings.

There are other acceptable frameworks; but to be complete, a reporter needs to cover all of those elements that apply to his study in some logical way. Various types of research will modify the requirements of a good report discussed in the following section, which is most closely aligned with reporting experimental studies. Not every report would have a separate section for each of the elements just listed; nor would every manuscript present them in the order given. The amount of flexibility in the prescription is controlled by the type of study, by its content, and by the needs of the selected audience. The important thing is that the researcher report clearly and completely, using *some* framework that is logical from the reader's point of view.

Elements in a good report

Good organization provides the framework for logical exposition and helps set up natural transition, but it cannot guarantee clear description within those parts. Each basic section that an effective research report normally includes should offer specific information; consequently, an analytic look at reporting, part by part, may be useful to the reporter.

Introducing the study

Most researchers understand the need for an introduction to their reports; but surprisingly often it is not their study they introduce to the reader but the general topic area in which the study takes place. This kind of background can be significant and a legitimate part of an introduction, but only after the reader is offered a statement of exactly what the study being reported did and is told about the problem that led to a rationale for the research. Some authors list hypotheses in the introduction, but usually they are given in a later section detailing the study. These primary elements of an introduction tell the reader what to expect from the report, whether he needs and wants to read it, and how the background material, which should follow, relates to the topic at hand.

Identification of the study at hand.   It seems obvious that the reader needs to know right off what the researcher did, but it is not unusual to come across manuscripts—and even published articles—in which the reader is strung along for 500 to 3,000 words before he is given the information. When the reader finally gets to this vital information, it is necessary for him to reread all the preceding pages in order to restructure the material with that focus. In a sense, the reader is doing this for the author, who failed to consider the reader's point of view.

Some authors argue that an accompanying abstract of their study suffices for an introductory explanation of the study, but a good abstract is written from a *completed* report, which is adequately introduced. The abstract is written in a very turgid, special language style and serves a different reader need than does the complete report; it is no more an introduction than is the title.

The rationale.   In the introductory section, the reporter must convey the importance of his study as it relates to any problems, questions, and theories which motivated it. In this section of a report—sometimes called the "background" of the research—the researcher needs to convince the reader that his study was worth doing. Otherwise, the reader can easily conclude that the merit for having conducted the study is either suspect or at least questionable. Such a discussion will occur as a part of one's rationale.

Some authors prefer to use the discussion of the rationale at the very beginning of the report followed by the initial description of the study. Others handle the rationale in a discreet subsection. Since the rationale is the resulting heart of the background material, it frequently involves some of the major related sources. If such sources cannot be treated separately from other related literature, the reporter is forced to combine the background with the related literature. In such a case, the reporter must write exceptionally clearly, identifying the rationale within the other background material.

Definition of terms.   When the terms in a study are unusual to the audience, applied to the study in any special way, affected by unresolved issues in the field, or unusually complicated, an early section defining terms will avoid confusion for the reader throughout the report.

A key for the reader.   In introducing the study, the author has the option of using the seemingly obvious but surefire technique of giving his reader a short itinerary of the ground that he will cover. A paragraph can key the reader to the major points to be considered and track him through the report. To do this, the author must have necessarily outlined the report, knowing clearly how it will develop and where the emphases will fall. Many authors avoid this approach as unworthy of polished exposition, but a report can be written without sounding as though it has been taken from an original proposal for the study. If, however, the skeletal words "This article reports a study which . . ." are followed by a billing so accurate and balanced that the reader never feels off the track throughout the article, the author could have done much worse.

Reviewing the literature

Of all the elements in a report, the section on related research or literature often proves the greatest challenge to the researcher's writing ability. Many reports prefer to include related literature as a part of a longer introduction; but particularly when there is a great deal of material to be covered, the analysis of it may stand as a subsection of the manuscript by itself. Some authors handle the review of related research as a beginning of the body of their report, and adept analysts may skillfully use a number of studies later in the report to help delineate aspects of their own research.

In presenting related research, the writer must call on his powers of selection and analysis in order to place the study being reported clearly against the background and in order to provide meaningful organization for the material in this section. This perspective is blurred if the author feels that, having selected a study for examination in the course of his own reading, he is obligated to summarize it for his readers whether it is relevant or not. Some authors find it difficult to select effectively for this section because their interest—or even their research—is broader than the areas they have chosen for their report. Such authors seem to be spurred to include as much tangential information as possible. This problem occurs frequently when unpublished authors adapt their dissertations for publication. A padded section of related literature would seem to confuse the reader about the relation of the study at hand to the background material.

A weak related literature section of a report can result when an author exercises no analytic lever on the material. Consequently, the related studies are presented in chronological order or are merely juxtaposed in no apparent order. One feels that he is reading a collection of loosely related abstracts. The best reviews of literature result from careful selection and are presented with an organization that is a product of the author's synthesis of what the related studies mean in terms of the study being reported. Almost always, the author who handles this section of the report skillfully also displays skillful writing and clear thinking throughout the report.

Another significant problem noted in the reporting of related literature is the failure to explain studies fully and/or clearly enough for the reader to grasp them. No study relevant enough to include should be presented to the reader in an unclear manner; but in too many reports, even major related studies are inadequately explained.

Describing the study in detail

The description of the study being reported often comes under one major heading. Such a section may include subsections on design, subjects, materials, and procedures; and a further breakdown may be used in describing these. What is important is that the description of the study be complete and logically presented, so that when the reader has finished reading it, he understands what was done. While the nature of the study being reported may account for variations in its description, it cannot excuse a lack of completeness or ambiguity. *This section, above all, must be crystal clear to the reader and must not raise any major questions.* The description of the study must give enough basic information for the reader to determine what is involved in replicating it.

Sometimes replication involves a quantity of detail that is available elsewhere: the reader can be referred to the exact content of a long questionnaire, for example. There is, however, nothing more frustrating for a reader than to be persuaded that a study is valid and then to find important information missing in the description of its design, materials, instruments, subjects, or procedures. The writer should never allow the reader to doubt the integrity of honest research because of vague or missing descriptions. Information muddled or omitted may include details that would reveal an inadequate sample or an untreated variable. The careful reader is not fooled when an author is, as one reviewer of a research manuscript once expressed it, "deplorably cavalier in providing less than the minimum information about the subjects used."

Some researchers use designs, instruments, and statistical approaches which are very sophisticated. Describing those aspects of such studies for the average reader of a research journal can be very difficult. Unless the researcher is communicating through a vehicle basically limited to readers at his own level of sophistication, however, the reporter is obligated to explain those aspects of his research so that a majority of his readers will understand his report. Tables and figures can be used to simplify the explanation, but the reporter must give the reader enough information in his exposition to read the tables and figures. Also, the reader can be referred to sources which detail the type of design.

A checklist of the elements in a complete section detailing a study includes careful descriptions of:

the hypotheses, if not used earlier in the report
the research design
the procedures followed in implementing the design
all instruments used in the study
the statistical techniques employed
the population studied and samples used
all steps followed in collecting the data

Considering the study's limitations

One of the surest signs of a careful researcher is the reporter who handles the limitations of his study openly. This section should be thorough and, after considering all the aspects of the design and procedures, include any weaknesses in samples, instruments, or design. Uncontrolled variables and any assumptions made in the study should be noted.

The reliable reporter will resist the temptation to dull the edge of this self-examination with vagueness; yet many authors are unable to broach this section at all, and when prompted to do so will interpret limitations as merely considering the limitations of extending the findings as implications. Wise researchers strengthen the real worth of their work with candid objectivity. On the basis of an open section on limitations, it can more readily be determined whether, with the acknowledged qualifications, the report of the research merits attention. Not including such a section does not mean that the limitations will not be considered without the author's acknowledgement; and the editor, reviewer, or reader who must make this evaluation alone is justifiably quite wary of the researcher who acknowledges no flaws in his or her work, suggesting that it is perfect.

There is no absolute prescription for placing limitations in a report. They can become a subsection or a separate unit in the report. Sometimes they follow the detailed description of the study. Often they are discussed after the findings are presented and before subsequent analysis of the findings. Some authors use them before or after a discussion of the implications; and although they are validly related to this element of the report, they tend to make a weak conclusion to a report when presented last.

Evaluating the results

One of the major problems that editors of research reports encounter is in helping authors clear up the evaluative discussions in their reports. It is particularly crucial that an author distinguish among findings and interpretations, conclusions, and implications in the report. Many writers confuse these and throw them into a *pot pourri* under the subtitle "Discussion." Too often the result is an uninterpretable mish mash. An author would be well advised to separate these elements and to present each as a distinct segment of the research report.

Findings and interpretations. The findings are often presented at the end of the major section describing the study, and the fact that they are *not* an evaluative element recommends this placement. When the findings are long and include numerous tables, they can be presented as a major section by themselves. But because all of the evaluative elements of the report are based on them, many authors begin their evaluative section with them. It is essential in doing so that the researcher let his findings stand free of his evaluative analysis, however.

In the section on findings, the writer simply reports what was found. Findings grow directly out of the implementation of the study. After presenting the findings, the author will then probably want to offer some explanation of why the study found what it did. These are interpretations of the findings and may logically appear in the same subsection.

Conclusions. Conclusions are developed *from* findings. They are the generalizations on the subject of the study that one can draw based on what has been discovered.

Implications. Implications are an author's estimate of what his findings and conclusions mean. The writer is, in effect, saying that if his findings and conclusions are accurate and acceptable, they then have certain implications for practice, for future research, or for theory development. Frequently authors equate implications with recommendations for future research, which is but a part of this opportunity to evaluate the findings. The researcher should determine if there are other implications as well.

As one experienced editor of reading research reports points out, "The exposition of each of these elements of the report should force the author to come to grips with himself and his study and to face several successive moments of truth."

Some specifics on writing

Once the writer has selected material so that it is clearly focused on the topic and audience, has ordered his material in a logically informative way, and has developed it completely, he will want to be sure his style is precise and easy to read and understand. Specific style problems frequently relate to narrower aspects of the language, such as word choice, sentence structure, and the way clauses, sentences, and ideas are connected.

Writing precisely and clearly

Diction. Although the nature of the content in research journals frequently is highly statistical, generally the diction of the better written articles is clear and simple without talking down to a knowledgeable audience. The terminology is usually standard to people in the field and need not, therefore, always be defined. If, however, the terms are new or perhaps are being used in a unique or different manner, definitions are called for. Perhaps the best advice might be, "When in doubt, define." Once this question of defining terms is settled, the writing in any publication should be clear to a neophyte.

Ideas that the language cannot handle with single terms have to be expressed with phrases; but occasionally a writer will abuse this language phenomenon and indulge in what a reviewer recently referred to as "glamorous terminology of the sort that theoretical sociologists enjoy using." An analysis of such diction reveals that the phrases it creates are often metaphors for ideas easily presented with simpler terms. Such diction is a kind of academic "poor poetry" which few readers are eager to explicate. When a report writer cannot resist creating unnecessary jargon, he has the obligation to clarify. But writers sometimes fail to define even necessary terms for the reader when they are first used and may fail to use the same terms throughout the report. Sometimes the same term is used with several distinct meanings. If the signals are mixed or unclear, communication will not take place.

Syntax. Frequently, problems with sentence structure in research manuscripts relate to length and to the way ideas are connected. Long sentences are often weak and suggest that a real problem is a frugal attitude on the part of the writer toward all the information he has gathered. In a kind of frenzy to get everything possible into a published article, a reporter may reveal a startling lack of understanding of the relevance of syntax to ideas. The number of misplaced and dangling or floating modifiers that are encountered in some manuscripts suggests that many writers expect their readers to do all the thinking by relating ideas that are merely juxtaposed.

Careless selection of joiners or omission of them altogether relates ideas obliquely to their real association, and the writer muffs the opportunity to communicate with exactness. Many writers give far too little thought to the precision of their conjunctions and prepositions. The joiner with the precise shade of meaning needed is overlooked in the writer's penchant for another word, which, overworked, creates monotony as well as a lack of clarity. Often in research reporting, numerical sequence is used rather than a more analytic transition between elements in a series of ideas. Writers might challenge their inclination to enumerate to be sure that counting is the best way to show how the ideas being counted relate.

Actually, any lack of appropriate grammatical relationship loses editors before readers, and unclear ideas should be either adequately related to or omitted from the exposition before publication. It is not surprising that—on being asked to rewrite unclear passages—many authors are quickly convinced that the sentences are not worth saving. Occasionally, an unclear clause in the original manuscript ends up as an important paragraph of its own in the rewrite.

Certainly, communicating ideas clearly is the objective of research reporting—not the display of sophisticated essay form. In this respect, writing a research report is different from literary writing. Although excellent exposition has its place in a research report, the purpose of research reporting must be to help the reader to understand the research and to evaluate its quality from the report. In a clearly written article— whether it is polished in style or not—reader attention is immediately focused on the specifics of the content.

Accuracy.   Although accuracy is not really a matter of style, it is the most universal specific requirement enforced on a manuscript. One discernible mistake in a published report can undermine the reader's entire confidence in the study because, as a reviewer has put it, it "may signal the presence of other careless errors that are not discoverable in the report." Accuracy requires vigilance. Every time material is copied—from notes or computer printout to handwritten drafts to typewritten drafts to final manuscripts—one must guard against the potential for inaccuracy.

The highest potential for outright inaccurate information in any manuscript is often in its reference list. If this part of a report is to serve its purpose as a tool for the reader, it must be accurate. It is the researcher's responsibility not to misdirect his reader by misspelling an author's name or by giving the wrong date, volume number, or page numbers. Such errors frequently occur in submitted manuscripts, and they shake one's confidence in the full report they document.

Using subheads

Many writers are perplexed by the need to identify the parts of their reports with internal headlines called subheads. These are not only attractive typographic devices, but they act as guideposts to the reader. Individual publications have unique formats which use different typefaces for various levels of subheads. A good reporter will know the various levels of subheads used by the publication he has selected as a target and will exploit the subhead device to reveal organization and to help the reader grasp the material. One way of doing this is to be sure the subheads used at each level are parallel in both importance and syntax. Subheads are sometimes merely labels of the standard parts or elements of the report, but the more informative subhead will also bill some of the specifics of the content in the segment it identifies. Since subheads are dividers, not joiners, the writer should not rely on subheads to replace transition between parts.

The use of subheads offers the writer an excellent opportunity to evaluate his organization. If, after completing the first draft of a report, the reporter lists the subheads used, indenting uniformly with each level, he will end up with a topical outline of the report. A quick examination of this outline will reveal 1) whether the report is logically ordered, 2) whether the parts of the report under major subheads are adequately parallel and those parts presented as a breakdown of each major part are adequately parallel, and 3) whether the parts of the report which should be parallel add up to convincing units.

The integrity of reporting

Writing style is highly individualistic; and this fact guarantees that careful consideration of the basic elements of research writing will result in better reports written in unique styles. Yet, the research report writer has the obligation to be clear and informative, to be precise and accurate, and to be thorough but relevant and concise. To be less than that is to fail himself, his research, and his reader. A good report will not cover up for a poor study, but a weak report can bury the best research.